PARIS

Date: 12/21/20

914.4361 FOD 2021
Dunlop, Fiona,
Fodor's 25 best. Paris /

D0115663

Contents

KEY TO SYMBOLS

- ➕ Map reference to the accompanying pull-out map
- ✉ Address
- ☎ Telephone number
- 🕐 Opening/closing times
- 🍽 Restaurant or café
- Ⓜ Nearest Métro (subway) station
- 🚌 Nearest bus route
- 🚆 Nearest rail station

ENTERTAINMENT 130

Whether you're after a cultural fix or just want a place to relax with a drink after a hard day's sightseeing, we've made the best choices for you.

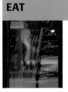

EAT 140

Uncover great dining experiences, from a quick bite at lunch to top-notch evening meals.

SLEEP 152

We've brought together the best hotels in the city, whatever budget you're on.

NEED TO KNOW 160

The practical information you need to make your trip run smoothly.

PULL-OUT MAP

The pull-out map with this book is a comprehensive street plan of the city, with a more detailed map of Montmartre on the back. We've given grid references within the book for each sight and listing.

- 🛥 Nearest riverboat or ferry stop
- ♿ Facilities for visitors with disabilities
- 🛈 Tourist information
- ❓ Other practical information
- 💷 Admission charges: Expensive (over €14), Moderate (€10–€14) and Inexpensive (under €10)
- ▷ Further information

Introducing Paris

The City of Light needs no introduction: the Eiffel Tower, Sacré-Cœur, the Louvre. It is not a museum, however, but a vibrant urban area. Most of the monuments won't change, but everything else will. Forget stereotypes and see the city with new eyes.

Paris has been making a concerted effort to change its image as a cold city full of rude, arrogant people. That reputation was never entirely deserved, but the good news for both visitors and residents is that Paris has undergone many changes for the better. The mayor's office and the national government sponsor a number of popular (and free) annual events along the lines of the *Fête de la Musique* (21 June), which bring the normally reserved Parisians out to have fun.

In addition to *Paris Plages*, when the Right Bank of the Seine becomes a sandy beach for one month in the summer, the city is the site of *La Nuit des Musées* (May), when several museums stay open all night; *Les Journées du Patrimoine* (September), when normally off-limits monuments are open; *La Nuit Blanche* (October), for all-night art and cultural events; and outdoor music concerts in the summer.

And Paris is no longer deserted in August. At one time it became a quiet village while the working population holidayed elsewhere, but the French now stagger their holidays. Paris in August is still quiet, but more restaurants and shops are open. Picnicking in the city is now popular and the banks of the Seine and parks are full of outdoor diners. The once-forbidden lawns in its parks and squares are packed with children and sunbathers enjoying the summer sun.

Most visitors come to see the great monuments, however. Having miraculously survived wars and revolution—some of them for a thousand years—the belief they are eternal was challenged by the fire at Notre-Dame in 2019.

Recently, much effort has gone into improving the quality of life in Paris, with projects like the Vélib' Métropole bicycle hire scheme (▷ 167) and *Paris Plages* enjoyed by Parisians and visitors alike.

FACTS AND FIGURES

- Population: 2.1 million
- Area: 105 sq km (40.5 sq miles)
- GDP (Île de France): 30 percent of the country's total GDP
- Highest spot: Montmartre (128m/420ft)
- Mayor: Anne Hildago (Socialist)
- Divided into 20 *arrondissements*
- Eiffel Tower: The tower has 2.5 million rivets and is lit by 20,000 light bulbs

FLIGHT OF FANCY

The first manned flight took place in Paris when Pilatre de Rozier and the Marquis d'Arlandes made a 25-minute trip in a hot-air balloon from the Bois de Boulogne to what is now the 13th *arrondissement* on 21 November 1783. Among the crowd observing their feat was none other than Benjamin Franklin, one of the founding fathers of the USA.

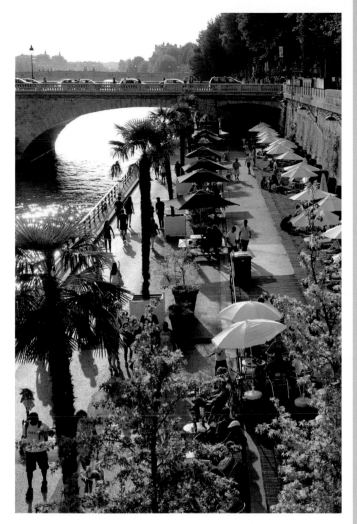

CLOSED

Each Tuesday a crowd of disappointed tourists gathers outside the closed entrance to the Louvre pyramid. Remember that most major museums are closed one day a week: Monday for the city-run museums (such as the Musée Carnavalet and Musée d'Art Moderne de la Ville de Paris) and Tuesday for national museums (including the Louvre, Centre Pompidou and Grand Palais).

DID YOU KNOW?

● Every evening, nearly 300 Parisian monuments, hotels, churches, fountains, bridges and canals are illuminated against the night sky.
● France has banned smoking inside restaurants, bars and cafés, for the dining pleasure of all.
● Watch your step! In spite of the city's best efforts to alleviate the problem, dog droppings are still a hazard.

Focus on the Movies

Few places are as closely associated with the film industry as Paris, the birthplace of cinema and a city whose many charms have been embedded in the world's imagination through the movies.

Birth of a New Medium

The history of modern cinema began properly in Paris on 28 December 1895, in the Salon Indien of the Grand Café on the boulevard des Capucines. At this venue, the Lumière brothers, Louis and Auguste, first demonstrated the potential of their invention, the *cinématographe*—a portable camera, film processing unit and projector combined—by screening 10 of their short films to a paying audience. The first film they showed was *La Sortie des Usines Lumière*, a simple shot of workers leaving the family's factory in Lyon. It lasted less than a minute, yet the public response was immediate and enthusiastic. A new entertainment medium had hit the scene, paving the way for one of the most influential and commercial entertainment genres for future generations.

The Parisian Scene

Throughout cinema history, Paris itself has been one of the great stars of the silver screen. In the 1926 silent film *Paris*, Charles Ray fell for Joan Crawford in the louche setting of the Paris Apache (pronounced Ah-Pahsh) or demi-monde, the era of hedonistic lifestyles and decadent jazz clubs. The Apaches were originally Paris members of street gangs, and later the name was used for a new dance. In the 1950s, a string of big-budget Hollywood movies, from *An American in Paris* (1951) to *Funny Face* (1957), peddled the image of Paris as the capital of love and romance to a receptive international audience, with gamine European actresses like Leslie Caron and Audrey

Clockwise from top: La Pagode cinema in rue de Babylone; Le Champo cinema in rue des Écoles; a scene from An American in Paris, 1951; Amélie, 2001,

Hepburn personifying its elegance and fashion sense. In *Sabrina* (1954), Hepburn can be seen composing a letter to the wistful tune of "La Vie en Rose" as the Sacré-Cœur is seen through an open window. The film and its content may only ever have been an outsider's ideal of the City of Light, but as myths go it was a potent one. Hepburn was a Parisian *ingénue* in *Love in the Afternoon* (1957) and returned for *Paris When it Sizzles* (1964), though by then, perhaps, the formula had become a little stale.

Beyond the Romance
Inevitably, the depiction of Paris in French cinema has been somewhat less starry-eyed. Jean-Luc Godard's *Breathless* (*À Bout de Souffle*; 1960) may have had the relationship between Jean-Paul Belmondo and Jean Seberg at its core, but this *nouvelle vague* masterpiece is no sugar-coated romance. François Truffaut's *The Last Metro* (1980) dealt with the perils of the German occupation, Cyril Collard's *Savage Nights* (1992) with the complications of love in a time of AIDS. But French cinema is not immune to the capital's charms either, as Jean-Pierre Jeunet's magical, color-saturated *Amélie* (2001) proved to huge international success. The film featured Audrey Tautou as a shy waitress in a Montmartre café, and Paris itself—as enchanting as in any 1950s musical—was her co-star.

The Tradition Maintained
Paris has remained true to its early passion for film. Director Luc Besson's project for La Cité du Cinéma (City of Cinema), which opened in 2012, has brought 45,000 sq m (484,400 sq ft) of film production space to a former power station in the northern suburb of Saint-Denis. The impact of film on the city comes full circle.

was filmed at the Les Deux Moulins café; a poster for the Lumière brothers' new world of cinema; at work on Paris When it Sizzles, *1964*

Top Tips For...

These great suggestions will help you tailor your ideal visit to Paris, no matter how you choose to spend your time. Each sight or listing has a fuller write-up elsewhere in the book.

Antiquing
Hunt for a bargain at the **Marché aux Puces de Saint-Ouen** (▷ 28–29), an immense weekend flea market.
Put in a bid for the unique items at **Drouot Richelieu auction house** (▷ 125).
Browse the vintage bookstores in **Passage Verdeau** (▷ 21).

Haute Couture
Explore the creative process at **Musée Yves Saint Laurent** (▷ 72).
Find a wide selection of designer clothing at the department stores **Le Bon Marché Rive Gauche** (▷ 124), **Galeries Lafayette** or **Printemps** (▷ 126, panel).
Shop at the global headquarters of iconic French labels **Dior** on avenue Montaigne (▷ 125) and **Cartier** at rue de la Paix (▷ 124).

Fine Dining
Check out the Michelin-starred **Gordon Ramsay au Trianon** (▷ 148), a luxurious dining experience, on a trip to Versailles.
Find out how **Guy Savoy** turns cooking into an art form at his eponymous restaurant (▷ 149).
Put yourself in the hands of chef Eric Frechon and try his tasting menu at **Epicure** (▷ 148).

All-Night Antics
Drink martinis into the wee hours in the old-fashioned New World ambience of **Harry's New York Bar** (▷ 137).
Gasp at the high-kicking routines at **Le Crazy Horse** cabaret show (▷ 136).

Clockwise from top: A market stall at the Marché aux Puces de Saint-Ouen; relaxing in the Jardin du Luxembourg; an art installation at the Musée d'Art

Descend into the medieval basement at **Caveau de la Huchette** for jazz (▷ 135). Take in a concert at the **Divan du Monde** (▷ 137) and afterwards hear some guest DJs.

Catering to the Kids
Ride the glass elevator to the top of the **Eiffel Tower** (▷ 60–61).
Explore interactive exhibitions at the **Cité des Sciences et de l'Industrie** (▷ 76).
Set the children loose in the **Si Tu Veux** toy shop (▷ 129).
See a dinosaur skeleton at the **Muséum national d'Histoire Naturelle** (▷ 72).

Shoestring Pleasures
Take advantage of free admission to the permanent collections of all city-run museums: the **Maison de Victor Hugo** at place des Vosges (▷ 53), the **Musée d'Art Moderne de la Ville de Paris** (▷ 69) and many more.
Visit the **Atelier Brancusi**, a reconstruction of sculptor Constantin Brancusi's workshop, in front of the **Centre Georges Pompidou** (▷ 16–17), for free.

Bird's-Eye Views
Check out the view from **Printemps de la Maison's** ninth floor (▷ 126, panel).
Take in the view from the terrace of **La Grande Arche** at La Défense (▷ 76).
Eat in the Eiffel Tower's **Le Jules Verne** restaurant (▷ 149) for fine food with views.

Lazy Mornings
Cruise leisurely down the Seine in a *bateau mouche* (▷ 58–59).
Commune with the ghosts of Sartre and Hemingway at the **Café de Flore** (▷ 66).
Sit by the fountain in the **Domaine nationale du Palais-Royal** (▷ 67) with a book by Colette, who once lived there.

Moderne de la Ville de Paris; Harry's New York Bar in rue Daunou; an impressive glass dome dominates the prestigious Galeries Lafayette department store

Timeline

INTRODUCING PARIS

BEFORE 1000

- The Celtic tribe of Parisii settles on Île de la Cité around 200BC.
- By AD100 the Roman city of Lutetia, later Paris, is growing fast.
- In 451 Sainte Geneviève saves Paris from the threat of Attila the Hun.

1163 The building of Notre-Dame starts.

1337–1453 Hundred Years' War between France and England.

1431 Henry VI of England is crowned king of France in Notre-Dame.

1437 Charles VII regains control of Paris.

1572 St. Bartholomew Massacre occurs during the Wars of Religion.

1682 Louis XIV and the court move to Versailles.

1700s Intellectuals, including Rousseau and Diderot, introduce radical new ideas during the Age of Enlightenment.

1789 Storming of the Bastille.

1792 Monarchy abolished; proclamation of the Republic.

1804 Napoleon crowned emperor.

1830 Bourbons overthrown; Louis-Philippe crowned.

1848 Revolution topples Louis-Philippe; Second Republic headed by Napoleon III, who is later crowned emperor.

REIGN OF TERROR

From 1793 to 1794 the Reign of Terror seized France, masterminded by the ruthless, power-crazed Jacobin leaders Maximilien Robespierre and Georges Jacques Danton. The king, Louis XVI, was convicted of treason and guillotined in January 1793, followed in October by his queen, Marie-Antoinette. By mid-1794 more than 18,000 people are estimated to have been beheaded in France.

The gardens at the Château de Versailles

The Consecration of the Emperor Napoleon, *by Jacques-Louis David*

1852–70 Baron Haussmann oversees the transformation of Paris.

1870–71 Paris besieged by Prussians, civil uprising of the Commune, Republic restored.

1889 Eiffel Tower is completed.

1900 First Métro line opens.

1914–18 Paris bombarded by German cannon.

1940 Nazis occupy Paris, followed by Liberation in 1944.

1958 De Gaulle heads Fifth Republic.

1977 Jacques Chirac is elected mayor (then president in 1995). Centre Georges Pompidou opens.

1981 Election of President Mitterrand. He initiates his *Grands Projets*—a new building scheme.

2002 First *Paris Plage*, in which riverside roads are closed in summer to create an urban beach on the banks of the Seine.

2014 Anne Hidalgo is elected the first female mayor of the city.

2015 Terrorist attacks shock the city, but 1.6 million people march through Paris in defense of liberty.

2017 Paris is chosen to be the host city for the 2024 Summer Olympic Games.

2019 Notre-Dame is partially destroyed by a major fire, with the roof and spire collapsing.

The Liberation of Paris, 1944

THE SEINE

The city's history has been inextricably linked with the River Seine since its earliest origins as a Gaulish village on the Île de la Cité, an islet in the river. The Seine represents the very lifeblood of Paris, flowing majestically through its heart, animating the city, defining the capital geographically and reflecting its history in the many fine buildings that line its banks. After centuries of pollution—when the river was used as a sewer—the Seine has been cleaned and its water is less polluted than it has been for years, although it's probably not a good idea to jump in for a swim.

Top 25

This section contains the must-see Top 25 sights and experiences in Paris. They are listed alphabetically, and numbered so you can locate them on the inside front cover.

TOP 25

HIGHLIGHTS

● Views from the terrace
● *La Marseillaise*, François Rude
● Tomb of the Unknown Soldier

TIP

● The museum has audio-visual displays illustrating major historical events and the construction of the Arc.

At the hub of Haussmann's web of twelve avenues, which reach out like tentacles toward the city beyond, this is the ultimate symbol of Napoleon's military pretensions and might. Climb the 284 steps to the terrace for superb views.

National symbol Napoleon conceived the Arc de Triomphe as a symbol of his military might in 1806 but it was finished only in 1836 by Louis-Philippe. Two centuries on and the colossal monument is still an iconic image of national pride. It plays a central role in many of France's key commemorations, including VE Day (8 May), Bastille Day (14 July) and Remembrance Day (11 November). Within its grounds are the Tomb of the Unknown Soldier, installed in 1921 after World War I, and a

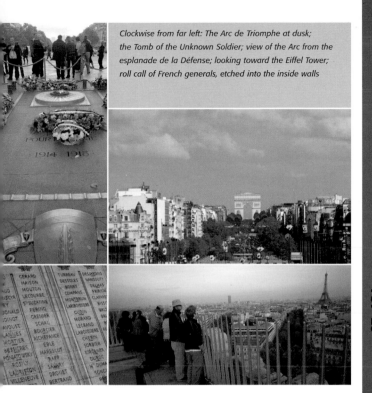

Clockwise from far left: The Arc de Triomphe at dusk; the Tomb of the Unknown Soldier; view of the Arc from the esplanade de la Défense; looking toward the Eiffel Tower; roll call of French generals, etched into the inside walls

poignant Memorial Flame, added two years later. This flame is rekindled every evening.

Special interest There are wonderful views from the rooftop, 50m (164ft) high. From here you can admire Haussmann's weblike street design and look along the Grand Axis toward place de la Concorde in one direction and the Grande Arche in the other. There is a small shop and museum on the way up. At ground level, admire the magnificent sculpted facade, the work of three artists. Don't miss the winged figure of Liberty on François Rude's sculpture *La Marseillaise*, calling the French to defend their nation (northeastern pillar, facing the Champs-Élysées). The 30 shields studding the crown of the arch each bear the name of a Revolutionary or Imperial victory.

THE BASICS

paris-arc-de-triomphe.fr

➕ B2

✉ Place Charles-de-Gaulle, 75008

☎ 01 55 37 73 77

🕐 Apr–Sep daily 10am–11pm; Oct–Mar 10am–10.30pm; times may vary. Last admission 45 mins before closing

Ⓜ Charles de Gaulle–Étoile

🚌 22, 30, 31, 52, 73, 92

♿ Moderate

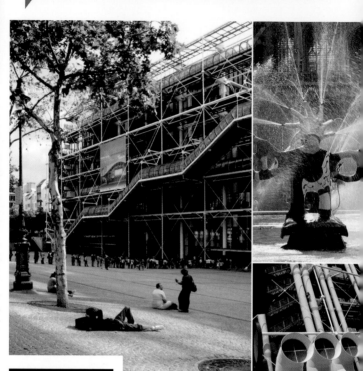

HIGHLIGHTS

● Design by Sir Richard Rogers, Renzo Piano and Jean-François Bodin
● View from the escalator
● Stravinsky fountain
● Stylish design in Georges restaurant
● *Avant-premières* (promotional events) for new and existing work of many top cinema directors
● Design shop on level 1

TIP

● Lines for tickets can be long; cut waiting times by booking in advance online.

Late opening hours make an exhibition visit possible between an *apéritif* and dinner in this controversial cultural area. Take your pick between the genesis of modernism, an art film or a drama performance.

High-tech culture More than a mere landmark in the extensive face-lift that Paris has undergone since the 1970s, the high-tech Centre Pompidou (known to Parisians as Beaubourg) is a hive of changing cultural activity. Contemporary art, architecture, design, photography, theater, cinema and dance are all represented, while the lofty structure offers exceptional views over central Paris. Take the transparent escalator tubes for a bird's-eye view of the piazza, where jugglers, artists, musicians and portrait artists perform for the crowds.

Clockwise from far left: The inside-out exterior; detail of the Stravinsky fountain; futuristic features on the exterior; glass corridor with fine views over the city; the Centre viewed above the rooftops; more pipes and structures on the facade

Classic modernism The Musée national d'Art Moderne's permanent collections feature work from 1905 to the 1960s on the fifth floor, with the contemporary collection on level four. Items displayed from the 59,000-strong collection change regularly and range from cubism by Georges Braque to Pop Art by Andy Warhol and video art by Korean artist Nam June Paik. For a chronological overview start on the fifth floor. Levels 1, 4 and 6 hold temporary exhibitions, while information libraries are on levels 1, 2 and 3. There are also cinemas on lower floors, and the restaurant Georges, with its wonderful views over the city, is on the top floor.

Renovation The exterior "caterpillar" staircase has recently been renovated, but the Centre remained open throughout the works.

THE BASICS

centrepompidou.fr

➕ K5

✉ Place Georges-Pompidou, 75004

☎ 01 44 78 12 33

🎨 Museum and exhibits Wed–Mon 11–9. Level 6 galleries close Thu 11pm. Atelier Brancusi (▷ 9) Wed–Mon 2–6. Library Mon, Wed–Fri 12–10, Sat–Sun 11–10

🍴 Georges restaurant on 6th floor; café

🚇 Rambuteau, Hôtel de Ville

🚌 20, 29, 32, 38, 39

🚆 RER Line A, B, Châtelet–Les Halles

♿ Excellent

👒 Moderate

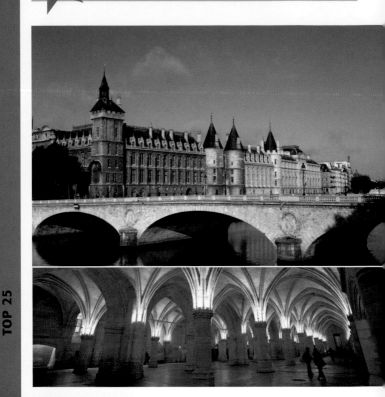

HIGHLIGHTS

- Marie-Antoinette's cell
- Tour Bonbec
- Prisoners' cells upstairs

TIP

- If you also plan to visit Sainte-Chapelle (▷ 56–57), go to the Conciergerie first and buy a joint ticket, to avoid the lines at Sainte-Chapelle. But do try to get to Sainte-Chapelle in the morning, before it gets very busy.

The ghosts of the victims of the guillotine must surely haunt this stark and gloomy place that served as a prison and torture chamber for more than five centuries. It remains full of macabre mementoes of its grisly past.

From palace to prison Rising over the Seine in menacing grandeur, the Conciergerie was built from 1299 to 1313 as part of a royal complex that also included Sainte-Chapelle. From 1391 until 1914 the building functioned as a prison and torture chamber, its reputation striking fear in the population. During the Revolution more than 2,700 people appeared before the Revolutionary Tribunal at the Conciergerie, including Marie-Antoinette and Maximilien Robespierre.

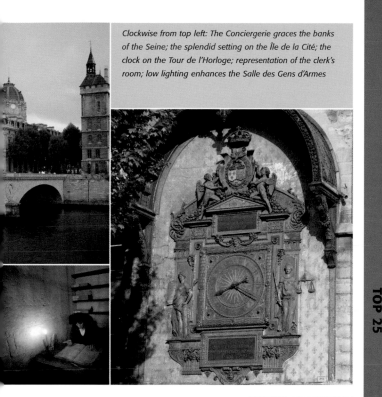

Clockwise from top left: The Conciergerie graces the banks of the Seine; the splendid setting on the Île de la Cité; the clock on the Tour de l'Horloge; representation of the clerk's room; low lighting enhances the Salle des Gens d'Armes

Relive history The boulevard du Palais entrance leads into the hauntingly lit Salle des Gens d'Armes. This hall is considered one of the finest examples of secular Gothic architecture in Europe. The curious spiral staircase on the right of the hall once led to the Great Ceremonial Hall on the upper floor of the palace. Off the Salle des Gens d'Armes is the gloomy Salle des Gardes; this acted as an antechamber to the now-vanished Grand'Chambre on the upper floor, where the Revolutionary Tribunal sat in 1793. Across the corridor known as the rue de Paris is the Galerie des Prisonniers, where lawyers, prisoners and visitors mingled. Here are re-creations of the concierge's and clerk's offices, as well as the Salle de Toilette, where prisoners were prepared for execution. At the far end is a poignant re-creation of Marie-Antoinette's cell.

THE BASICS

paris-conciergerie.fr

➕ J6

✉ 2 boulevard du Palais, Île de la Cité, 75001

☎ 01 53 40 60 80

🕐 Daily 9.30–6 (ticket office 5.30); times may vary

🚇 Cité, Châtelet

🚌 21, 38, 47, 75, 96

🎫 Inexpensive (joint ticket with Sainte-Chapelle expensive)

❓ Self-guided Histopad (tablet with tour app) inexpensive

4 Galerie Vivienne and the Passages Couverts

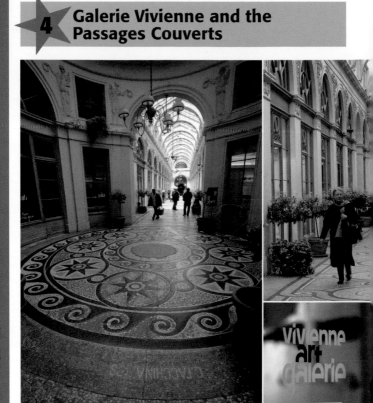

HIGHLIGHTS

- Mosaic floor, Galerie Vivienne
- Stamp dealers
- La Galerie Fayet
- Vintage children's books
- Decor, Le Grand Colbert

Centered on the 2nd *arrondissement* is a hidden network of interconnecting 19th-century shopping arcades or *passages couverts* that let you stroll under cover most of the way from the Palais Royal to the Grands Boulevards and beyond.

Galerie Vivienne Between the late 18th and early 19th centuries the Right Bank included a network of 140 covered passageways—the fashionable shopping malls of the time. Of those that survive, the Galerie Vivienne (1823) is perhaps the most glamorous, squeezed in between the Bibliothèque Nationale and the place des Victoires. You can track down designer clothes—Jean-Paul Gaultier was one of the first to open a shop here—or shop for unusual toys. It's perfect for a rainy day.

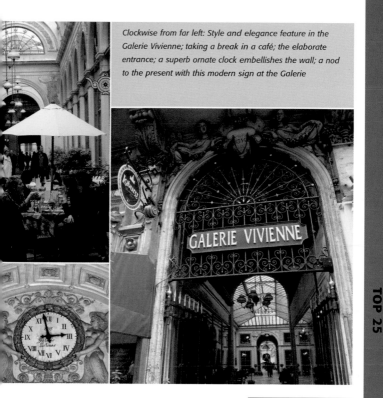

Clockwise from far left: Style and elegance feature in the Galerie Vivienne; taking a break in a café; the elaborate entrance; a superb ornate clock embellishes the wall; a nod to the present with this modern sign at the Galerie

Galerie Colbert Galerie Vivienne's nearby neighbor Galerie Colbert (1826) is as elegant, but lacks shops as it is part of the Institut national de l'Histoire de l'Art. Don't miss the 19th-century brasserie, Le Grand Colbert.

More offbeat browsing These interlinked arcades thread their way north from rue Saint-Marc across the boulevard de Montmartre and into the 9th *arrondissement*. The labyrinthine Passage des Panoramas (1800) is a little tired in places but full of inexpensive restaurants and stamp dealers. Facing it across boulevard de Montmartre is the Passage Jouffroy (1845), where the quirkiest of the boutiques, La Galerie Fayet, sells antique walking canes (▷ 126). Farther north still, the quieter Passage Verdeau (1847) has vintage book dealers.

galerie-vivienne.com

➕ H4–H3

✉ Galerie Vivienne: 4 rue des Petits-Champs/6 rue Vivienne, 75002

🍴 Bars and restaurants: Passages des Panoramas, 10 rue Saint-Marc, 75002

🚇 Bourse, Palais-Royal, Grands Boulevards

🚌 20, 29, 39, 48, 67, 74, 85

♿ Good

Ⓤ Free

5 Les Invalides

- The tomb of Napoleon
- Military architecture on a monumental scale
- Suit of armor belonging to King Henry II
- *Napoleon I on his Imperial Throne,* by Ingres
- The bugle that signaled the armistice at the end of WW1
- Enigma cryptography machine from WWII

TIP

- The museum app provides useful background information to the displays.

Also known as Hôtel national des Invalides, this splendid complex still provides care and shelter for France's military veterans. But it's best known around the world as the resting place of one of the country's most famous sons, Napoleon Bonaparte.

History of the complex In 1670 King Louis XIV commissioned architect Liberal Bruant to build the hospital to look after wounded soldiers and to provide shelter for homeless veterans. The massive complex, measuring 196m (643ft) along its river frontage, was finished in 1708.

Musée de l'Armée Les Invalides is home to the Army Museum, one of the largest museums devoted to military history in the world. Created in 1905, the collection is divided into several

Clockwise from far left: The majestic Église du Dôme; a fresco by Charles de la Fosse inside the church's cupola; Les Invalides by night; the square facing the Cour d'Honneur (Court of Honor); Napoleon's tomb in the Église du Dôme

departments. Lovers of late medieval history will enjoy the section relating to weapons of the 13th to the 17th centuries, while the most modern exhibitions concentrate on 1871 to 1945, the era that shaped contemporary Europe, including the two World Wars. There's a gallery here devoted to the wartime leader Charles de Gaulle.

Tomb of Napoleon Napoleon Bonaparte died in exile on the remote island of St Helena in 1821. His ashes were returned to France in 1840 and interred here in 1861, 40 years after his death. The Dôme des Invalides was built as the royal chapel of the Invalides complex. The tomb of red quartzite set atop a green granite base takes center stage in the rotunda. Visitors view the tomb from a marble gallery.

THE BASICS

musee-armee.fr
🞢 D6
✉ 129 rue de Grenelle, 75007
☎ 01 44 42 38 77
🕓 Jul–Aug daily 10–6, dome and tomb also Tue 10–9 and Thu 10–7; Apr–Jun, Sep daily 10–6, dome and tomb also Tue 10–9; Oct daily 10–6; Nov–Mar daily 10–5
🍴 Restaurant/Bar Le carré des Invalides
🚇 La Tour Maubourg, École Militaire, Varenne
🚌 83, 87, 93
♿ Good
❓ Downloadable app, concert season
✋ Moderate

HIGHLIGHTS

● Médicis fountain
● Musée du Luxembourg
● Bandstand
● Statue of Delacroix
● Orangerie
● Experimental orchard
● Beekeeping school
● Statues of queens
of France

Despite the crowds, these gardens are serene in all weathers and are the epitome of French landscaping. This idealized image of an unhurried Parisian existence is a world away from the big-city bustle nearby.

Layout Radiating from the large octagonal pond in front of the Palais du Luxembourg (now the Senate) are terraces, paths and a wide tree-lined alley that leads down to the Observatory crossroads. Natural attractions include shady chestnuts, potted orange and palm trees, an orchard and tropical hothouses. Statues of the queens of France and artists and writers are dotted about.

Park activities All year round, joggers pound the circumference and, in summer, sunbathers

Clockwise from far left: Strolling in front of the Palais du Luxembourg; detail of the Médicis fountain; relaxing in the gardens; bronze statue, l'Acteur Grec, by Charles-Arthur Bourgeois; the gardens provide the perfect setting for a game of chess

settle into chairs or lie on the grass, card- and chess-players claim the shade in front of the Orangerie, bands tune up at the bandstand near the boulevard Saint-Michel entrance and children burn off energy on swings and donkey rides. Fountains, tennis courts, beehives, a puppet theater and children's playgrounds offer other distractions. In the northwest corner of the park is Paris's oldest public museum, the Musée du Luxembourg. Opened in 1750, it became the first contemporary art museum in 1818 and today stages major temporary exhibitions of art.

Inspiration The Palais du Luxembourg and gardens were commissioned by Marie de Médicis, wife of Henri IV, in 1615, and designed to resemble her childhood Florentine home.

THE BASICS

🚇 G8/H8

✉ Main entrance place Edmond Rostand, 75006

☎ Park 01 42 34 20 00. Musée du Luxembourg 01 40 13 62 00, museeduluxembourg.fr

🕐 Park daylight hours. Museum daily 10–7.30 (until 10pm Mon and Fri)

🍴 Open-air café, kiosk

🚇 Odéon

🚌 21, 38, 58, 82, 84, 85, 86, 87, 89, 93 to museum

🚉 RER Line B, Luxembourg

♿ Very good

💰 Park free; museum moderate

7 Jardin des Tuileries

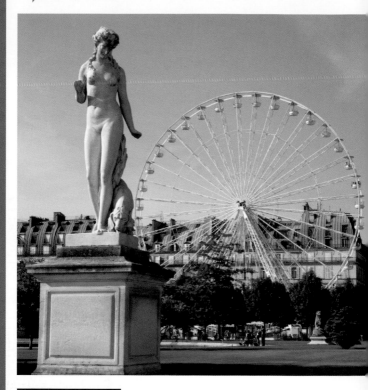

HIGHLIGHTS

- Jeu de Paume
- Orangerie
- Outdoor sculptures
- Views

Forming a verdant link between the Louvre and the Champs-Élysées, the Jardin des Tuileries is perhaps Paris's most visited green space. Here history meets contemporary life as office workers eat lunch and families relax among the fine formal gardens that started life as a private park for the French royal family.

Good views This is also a place from where visitors can see several of the city's main attractions. There are good views of the Louvre, the Eiffel Tower, the Musée d'Orsay across the river and up to the Arc de Triomphe at the top of the Champs-Élysées.

Design notes The formal design of the gardens can be credited to the landscape

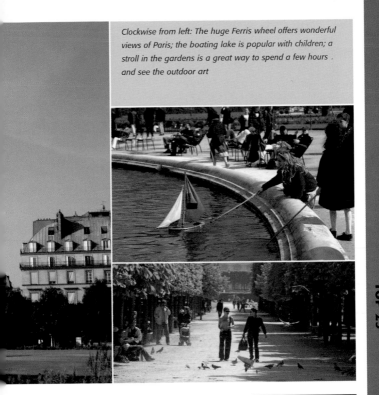

Clockwise from left: The huge Ferris wheel offers wonderful views of Paris; the boating lake is popular with children; a stroll in the gardens is a great way to spend a few hours and see the outdoor art

architect André le Nôtre, who was gardener to King Louis XIV and the man responsible for the spectacular gardens at Versailles. Le Nôtre laid out the Tuileries in 1664, and over 350 years later they are still being enjoyed.

Activities In one corner is a boating pond, and at the opposite end, overlooking the place de la Concorde, are two of the city's finest small galleries, the Orangerie (▷ 71–72) and the Jeu de Paume (▷ 51). The latter gets its name from the fact that it was once a real tennis court (*jeu de paume*) and the former a warm winter home for the orange trees from the Jardin. There is plenty of outdoor art in the gardens, too. Works by Giacometti, Rodin and Henry Moore are on display, along with several bronzes by Aristide Maillol.

THE BASICS

- F4–5/G4–5
- 113 rue de Rivoli, 75001
- Jun–Aug daily 7am–11pm; Apr–May, Sep 7am–9pm; Oct–Mar 7.30–7.30
- Cafés
- Tuileries
- 21, 27, 39, 67, 69, 72, 74, 95
- Good
- Free

HIGHLIGHTS

● Marché Serpette: art, high-quality furniture
● Marché Paul Bert: trendy items, including classic modern furniture
● Marché Jules Vallès: bric-a-brac
● Marché Biron: antiques, glass, art deco

TIP

● The market area is very extensive, so pick up a free map from the tourist office at 7 impasse Simon by the Marché Paul Bert.

A Sunday pastime popular with many locals is to look for bargains at the city's flea markets, of which the *crème de la crème* is still this one. Nowhere else will you find such a fascinating cross-section of Parisian society.

Duck and banter The approach from the Métro station to this sprawling 7ha (17-acre) market is uninspiring as it entails bypassing jeans and sportswear stalls before ducking under the Périphérique overpass and finally entering the fray. Persevere and you may discover an antique gem, a fake or a second-hand item. If your budget won't stretch to that, you can choose an old postcard of Paris from the thousands on show. Everything and anything is displayed here and all commerce is carried on in the true bantering style of the

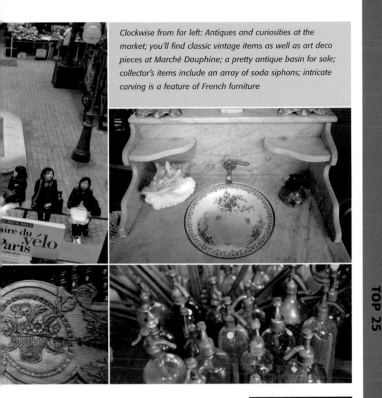

Clockwise from far left: Antiques and curiosities at the market; you'll find classic vintage items as well as art deco pieces at Marché Dauphine; a pretty antique basin for sale; collector's items include an array of soda siphons; intricate carving is a feature of French furniture

faubourgs. It pays to get "creatively lost," since the most intriguing vendors are not necessarily the ones with the most prominent sites. In particular, don't miss the upper level if you're visiting the Marché Dauphine.

Bargain hard Registered dealers are divided into more than a dozen official markets, which interconnect through busy passageways. Along the fringes are countless hopefuls who set up temporary stands to sell goods ranging from obsolete kitchenware to old jukeboxes and junk. Although unashamedly a tourist trap, there is something for everyone here, but do go early. Bargaining is obligatory. Stop for lunch in one of the bistros along the rue des Rosiers or try the terrace of the café-theater A Picolo at 58 rue Jules-Vallès, which has occasional jazz concerts.

THE BASICS

marcheauxpuces-saintouen.com

➕ See map ▷ 115

✉ Porte de Clignancourt, 75018

☎ 01 40 11 77 36

🕐 Sat 9–6, Sun 10–6, Mon 10–5 (reduced hours in Aug)

🍽 Cafés and restaurants on rue des Rosiers

Ⓜ Porte de Clignancourt

🚌 56, 85

♿ Good

❓ Beware of pickpockets

9 Musée de Cluny – Musée national du Moyen-Âge

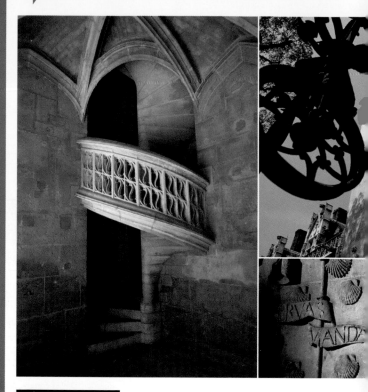

HIGHLIGHTS

● *La Dame à la Licorne* tapestries
● *Pilier des Nautes*
● Stone heads from Notre-Dame
● Medieval gardens
● Seventh-century crown
● Stained glass
● Abbot's Chapel

TIP

● The museum is closed for restoration until 2021 but the Roman baths and 70 artworks are on display.

Pause outside the ultra-contemporary entrance, surrounded by re-created medieval gardens, and prepare to enter a time warp that conjures up the days of troubadours and courtly love.

Treasures The Gothic, turreted Hôtel de Cluny was built at the end of the 15th century by Abbot Jacques d'Amboise and is one of France's finest examples of domestic architecture of this period. The museum it houses, also known as the Musée de Cluny, has 23,000 objects in its collection, most amassed by Alexandre du Sommerard, a 19th-century medievalist. The most famous exhibits are the beautiful *La Dame à la Licorne* tapestries (late 15th century). Costumes, accessories, textiles and tapestries are of Byzantine, Coptic or European

Clockwise from far left: Stone staircase, bathed in lights, in the Gothic Hôtel de Cluny; exterior of the building, now housing the museum; detail of a religious painting displayed in the museum; exterior courtyard, once the site of ancient Roman baths; detail of shells on the exterior

origin, while the gold and metalwork room has outstanding pieces of Gallic, Barbarian, Merovingian and Visigothic artistry. Room VIII houses 21 stone heads knocked from statues on the west front of Notre-Dame. Stained glass, table games, ceramics, wood carvings, illuminated manuscripts and Books of Hours, altarpieces and religious statuary complete this exceptional display.

Baths The late-Roman baths of Lutetia, which comprise cold (frigidarium), tepid (tepidarium) and hot (caldarium) rooms, form part of the museum complex. The most substantial surviving element is the frigidarium, whose restored 14.7m (48ft) vaulted ceiling, makes it one of the most important structures from antiquity to survive north of the Loire.

THE BASICS

musee-moyenage.fr

➕ J7

✉ 6 place Paul-Painlevé, 75005

☎ 01 53 73 78 00

🕐 Wed–Mon 9.15–5.45. Last admission 5.15

Ⓜ Cluny–La Sorbonne

🚌 21, 27, 38, 63, 85, 86, 87

🚆 RER Line B, Cluny

♿ Moderate during restorations; free first Sun of month

❓ Renovations ongoing. Guided tours: tel 01 53 73 78 16

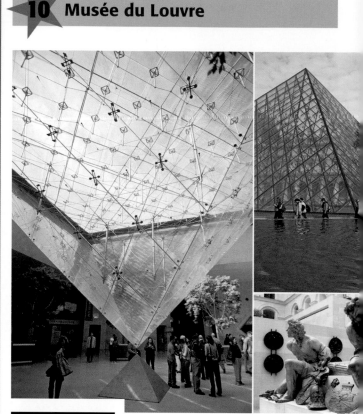

HIGHLIGHTS

- Palace of Khorsabad
- Glass pyramid entrance, designed by I.M. Pei
- *Bataille de San Romano*, Uccello
- *Mona Lisa*, da Vinci
- Napoleon III apartments
- Vénus de Milo
- Cour Carrée at night
- The Marly Horses

TIP

- To avoid the crowds, visit early morning or Wednesday or Friday evening.

Nocturnal lighting transforms the Louvre's glass pyramid entrance into a gigantic cut diamond—just a foretaste of the treasures contained within.

The world's largest museum Originally a medieval fortress, the Louvre first took shape as a private art gallery under François I, eager to display his Italian loot. Henri IV added several galleries, completed in 1610. After escaping the excesses of the Revolutionary mob, it became a people's museum in 1793 and was later enlarged by Napoleon I, who also enriched its collection. Today the Louvre remains a vibrant and exciting art gallery. Its star attraction, the iconic *Mona Lisa,* hangs in its own room which has been specially refurbished to make viewing the painting easier.

Clockwise from far left: All glass and light, the interior of the Louvre; a view across the fountains to the famous glass pyramid; The Raft of the Medusa by Théodore Géricault; detail of the glass pyramid; sculptures in the Richelieu Wing

Art fortress The vast collection of some 35,000 exhibits is arranged on four floors of three wings: Sully (east), Richelieu (north) and Denon (south), while beneath the elegant Cour Carrée lies the keep of the original medieval fortress. Almost 5,000 years of art are covered at the museum, starting with Egyptian antiquities and culminating with European painting up to 1848. Islamic art from three continents is showcased in a contemporary space within the Cour Visconti.

Making the most of your visit Buy your ticket online beforehand to avoid a long wait. You will not be able to see everything in one visit, so be selective. The free museum map, available from the information desk, highlights the key works and is useful when planning your visit.

THE BASICS

louvre.fr

🚇 H5

✉ 99 rue de Rivoli, 75058. Enter via Pyramid or Carrousel

☎ Information line 01 40 20 53 17; main line 01 40 20 50 50

🕐 Wed–Mon 9–6 (until 9.45pm Wed, Fri, first Sat of month)

🍴 Restaurants and cafés

🚇 Palais-Royal–Musée du Louvre

🚌 21, 27, 29, 39, 58, 67, 69, 70, 72, 74, 85, 95

♿ Excellent

💰 Expensive; temporary exhibitions expensive; free first Sat of month 6pm–9.45pm and first Sun of month Oct–Mar

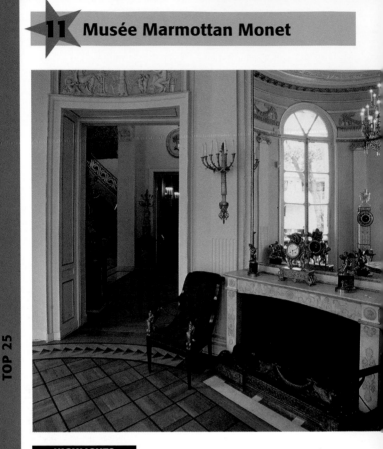

HIGHLIGHTS

- *Impression—soleil levant*, Monet
- Gold table-tray
- *Promenade près d'Argenteuil*, Monet
- *Charing Cross Bridge*, Monet
- *L'Allée des Rosiers*, Monet
- *Le Pont Japonais*, Monet
- Monet's *Water Lilies* series
- Monet's spectacles

The Marmottan Monet Museum, in the residential 16th *arrondissement*, houses a mesmerizing collection of Monet paintings, including many colorful canvases of the artist's home in Giverny.

Rich donations This often overlooked treasure of Parisian culture offers an eclectic collection built up over the years from the original dona-tion of Renaissance and First Empire paintings and furniture bequeathed by the art historian Paul Marmottan in 1932. His elegant 19th-century mansion, furnished with Renaissance tapestries and sculptures and Napoleonic furniture, was later given an extra boost by the stunning Wildenstein collection of 313 pages from illustrated manuscripts from the 13th to the 16th centuries, as well as an exceptional

Clockwise from far left: An elegant salon used to display Impressionist paintings; visitors admiring the works of Claude Monet and his contemporaries; the spacious rooms show Monet's paintings to their best advantage

donation from Michel Monet of works by his father Claude, the Impressionist painter. Other generous donations include works by Monet's contemporaries Gauguin, Renoir, Boudin, Pissarro, Sisley, Berthe Morisot and Gustave Caillebotte, but it is Monet's canvases of dappled irises, wisteria and water lilies, from his last years at Giverny, that are among the most sought out and memorable.

Visiting the museum The museum shop and Salons Impressionnistes are on the ground floor. You will find more Impressionists and the Salle Monet in the basement, while the Wildenstein collection of illuminated manuscripts is housed in a specially designed room. The museum also stages temporary exhibitions on themes related to its collections.

THE BASICS

marmottan.fr
➕ See map ▷ 114
✉ 2 rue Louis-Boilly, 75016
☎ 01 44 96 50 33
🕓 Tue–Sun 10–6 (Thu until 9). Last admission 30 mins before closing
🚇 La Muette
🚌 22, 32, 52, 63
🚆 RER Line C, Boulainvilliers
♿ Moderate

12 Musée national Picasso-Paris

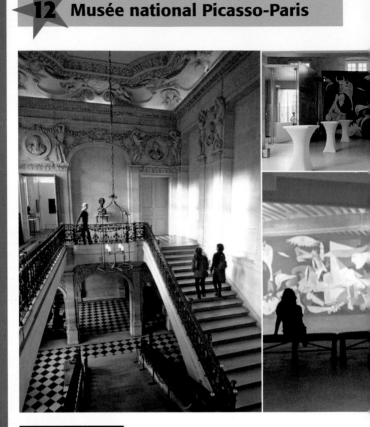

HIGHLIGHTS

● Ceramics
● *Man with a Guitar*
● Studies for *Les Demoiselles d'Avignon*

TIP

● The museum operates alongside other domestic and international cultural institutions, donating works for temporary exhibitions. As a result, gallery displays will change periodically.

Housing the largest collection of works by Picasso in the world, the Picasso Museum showcases the immense breadth of the artist and, with the art and objects he chose himself, offers an insight into the man.

Taxes After Picasso died in 1973, his family owed about $50 million in death duties. In lieu of this they gave the state 203 of Picasso's paintings, 158 sculptures and many other items including curios he had collected and paintings by other artists. When his widow died in 1986, further works were handed over. The result forms the basis of this remarkable collection covering all periods of the artist's life.

Hôtel Salé The building itself is a delight, originally built in the 1650s by a man who

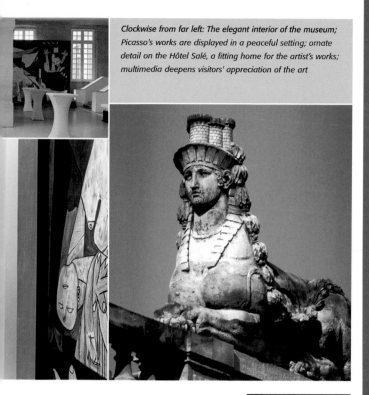

Clockwise from far left: The elegant interior of the museum; Picasso's works are displayed in a peaceful setting; ornate detail on the Hôtel Salé, a fitting home for the artist's works; multimedia deepens visitors' appreciation of the art

gained his own wealth from collecting the very unpopular salt tax that was levied in France at the time. In 1968 it was declared a historic monument, and it opened as the Musée Picasso in 1985. In the last several years the museum has undergone a $62-million renovation that has greatly enhanced the visitor experience.

The collection Spread over three floors, the collection does not contain the artist's best-known works, such as *Guernica*, but displays many works that he wanted to keep for himself. After all, he once declared himself the greatest collector of Picassos in the world. Works ranging from his Blue Period through to cubism and surrealism showcase the astonishing range of his talents.

THE BASICS

museepicassoparis.fr

✚ L5

✉ Hôtel Salé, 5 rue de Thorigny, 75003

☎ 01 85 56 00 36

🕐 Daily 9.30–6. Last admission 45 mins before closing

🍴 Café

🚇 Saint-Paul, Saint-Sébastien–Froissart

♿ Very good

❓ Audioguide. Tours in English on Sundays

✋ Moderate; free first Sun of the month

HIGHLIGHTS

● *Olympia*, Edouard Manet
● *Déjeuner sur l'Herbe*, Edouard Manet
● *Les Joueurs de Cartes*, Paul Cézanne
● *La Mère*, James McNeill Whistler
● *L'Angélus*, Jean-François Millet
● *La Cathédrale de Rouen*, Claude Monet
● *Dans un Café*, Edgar Degas
● *La Chambre à Arles*, Vincent van Gogh
● *Femmes de Tahiti*, Paul Gauguin
● Chair by Charles Rennie Mackintosh

TIP

● A Paris Museum Pass (▷ 170) allows you to skip the lines for tickets.

You'll either love or hate the conversion of this 1900 train station. But whatever your view, its art collections, covering the years from 1848 to 1914, are a must for anyone interested in this crucial art period.

Monolithic When this museum finally opened in 1986 controversy ran high: Gae Aulenti's heavy stone structures lay unhappily under Laloux's delicate iron-and-glass shell, built as a train terminus in 1900. But the collections redeem this faux pas, offering a solid overview of the momentous period from Romanticism to Fauvism. Works by the giants of French art—Degas, Monet, Cézanne, Van Gogh, Renoir, Sisley and Pissarro—are the biggest crowd pullers. The opulent restaurant of the old Hôtel d'Orsay on the first floor is a historic monument.

Clockwise from far left: Check out the view through the giant clock in the museum's café; memories of a train station are evoked on the vast ground floor; the ornate station clock; the Musée d'Orsay sits elegantly beside the River Seine

Other highlights You can also see paintings that are examples of Naturalism, Symbolism and the Nabis School. There are sculptures by Rodin, Émile-Antoine Bourdelle and Aristide Maillol, and art nouveau furniture. Save time for the Salle des Fêtes (room 51), tucked away at the end of the middle level. The extravagantly mirrored room with its many chandeliers was originally part of the station's hotel.

Take a tour The chronological tour of the gallery starts with the Impressionists (including Manet, Degas, Monet, Renoir and Sisley) on Level 5, with Post-impressionists (including Van Gogh, Gauguin and Seurat) on the median level below, along with a sculpture gallery. A strong program of temporary exhibitions enhances the permanent collection.

THE BASICS

musee-orsay.fr

✚ F5

✉ 62 rue de Lille, 75007

☎ 01 40 49 48 14

🕐 Tue–Sun 9.30–6 (Thu until 9.45pm)

🍴 Restaurant on first floor; Café Campana and Café de l'Ours

🚇 Solférino

🚌 24, 63, 68, 69, 73, 83, 84, 94

🚊 RER Line C, Musée d'Orsay

♿ Excellent

💰 Moderate; free first Sun of the month

❓ Audio and guided tours, concerts and lectures

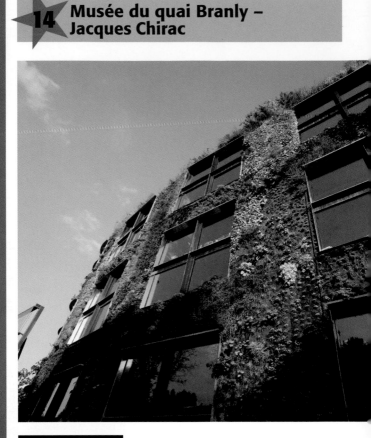

HIGHLIGHTS

● A glass tower of 9,000 musical instruments
● Nepalese ritual lamp
● Aztec statues
● The Harter bequest of masks and sculptures from Cameroon

TIP

● The museum gardens are particularly magical in the evening, when they are beautifully illuminated.

This eye-catching museum, founded by former French President and Mayor of Paris Jacques Chirac, is dedicated to the cultural heritage of Africa, Asia, Oceania and the Americas.

A 21st-century venue Built on five levels and crowned by a wide terrace with fine views of the Eiffel Tower, the museum is hidden from view by trees and thick vegetation. *Le mur végétal* (plant wall) on the north facade is festooned with 15,000 plants representing 150 species from all over the world.

The collection A swooping white ramp leads through a tunnel to the display area, where you are greeted by a 10th-century anthropomorphic Dogon wood statue from Mali, its one

Clockwise from far left: Plants from all over the world cover the exterior of the museum; head of a figurine from Ifa, Nigeria, dating from the 12th to 14th century; Oceania Gallery; Uli wooden sculpture, 18th to early 19th century, from New Ireland, Oceania

remaining arm reaching skywards. This splendid beginning sets the tone for other highlights, including painted animal hides from the Americas, decorated with battle scenes and abstract earth and sky motifs; a glass tower of 9,000 musical instruments gathered from all corners of the world; and a headdress from Malekula Island, worn by dancers during rituals in the early 20th century. To aid navigation through the museum, each of the different regions has its own floor coloring.

Other attractions The museum stages several temporary exhibitions each year, as well as drama, dance and music in the theater, and hosts debates on historic and contemporary issues. It also has a cinema and holds regular hands-on workshops for adults and children.

THE BASICS

quaibranly.fr

🚪 B5

✉ 37 quai Branly, 75007 (also 218 rue de l'Université)

☎ 01 56 61 70 00; Ticketline 01 56 61 71 72

🕐 Sun, Tue–Wed 11–7, Thu–Sat 11–9

🍴 Les Ombres (on the roof terrace, tel 01 47 53 68 00) and Café Jacques (in the garden)

🚇 Alma–Marceau

🚌 43, 63, 72, 80, 87, 90

🚆 RER Line C, Pont de l'Alma

♿ Good

✋ Inexpensive; gardens free

★15 Musée Rodin

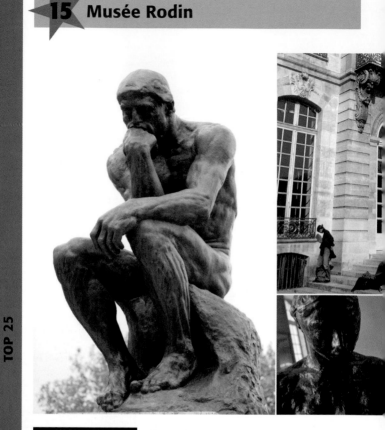

HIGHLIGHTS

- Les Bourgeois de Calais (The Burghers of Calais)
- Le Penseur (The Thinker)
- La Porte de l'Enfer (The Gates of Hell)
- Le Baiser (The Kiss)
- La Main de Dieu (The Hand of God)
- Adam et Eve
- Ugolin
- Le Père Tanguy, Van Gogh
- Original staircase

The enchanting Musée Rodin showcases an outstanding collection of the popular artist's work as well as representations of some of his contemporaries.

Hard times Built in 1730, the rococo Hôtel Biron, which houses the Rodin museum, has an interesting history. One owner (the Duc de Lauzun) was sent to the guillotine and the house has been used successively as a dance hall, convent, school and artists' studios. Rodin lived here from 1908 until his death in 1917. In 1919 the house became a museum and, despite its chequered history, is an impressive gallery space befitting Rodin's stature as an influential French sculptor. The renovated chapel in the grounds is used for temporary art and sculpture exhibitions.

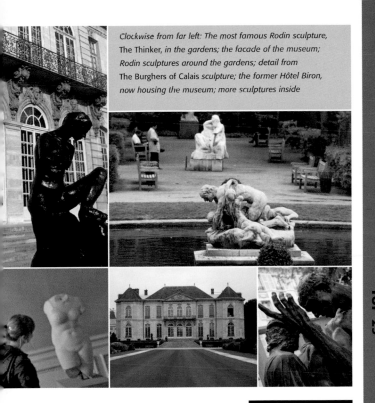

Clockwise from far left: The most famous Rodin sculpture, The Thinker, in the gardens; the façade of the museum; Rodin sculptures around the gardens; detail from The Burghers of Calais sculpture; the former Hôtel Biron, now housing the museum; more sculptures inside

Sculpture The elegant, luminous interior houses the collection that Rodin left to the nation. It ranges from his early sketches to the later watercolors and includes many of his most celebrated white marble and bronze sculptures, including *The Kiss* (*Le Baiser*). There are busts of the composer Mahler and writer Victor Hugo, among others, and studies of Balzac. Alongside the Rodins are examples of work by his peers, in particular his mistress and model, Camille Claudel, as well as Carrière, Munch, Renoir, Monet and Van Gogh. Rodin's furniture and antiques complete this exceptional collection.

Retreat The museum's private gardens cover 3ha (7.5 acres) and contain several major sculptures, a pond, flowering shrubs and benches for a quiet read.

THE BASICS

musee-rodin.fr
✚ E6
✉ 79 rue de Varenne, 75007
☎ 01 44 18 61 10
🕐 Tue–Sun 10–6.30. Last admission an hour before closing
🍽 Peaceful garden café
🚇 Varenne, Invalides
🚌 69, 82, 87, 92
🚊 RER line C, Invalides
♿ Wheelchair access
💰 Moderate

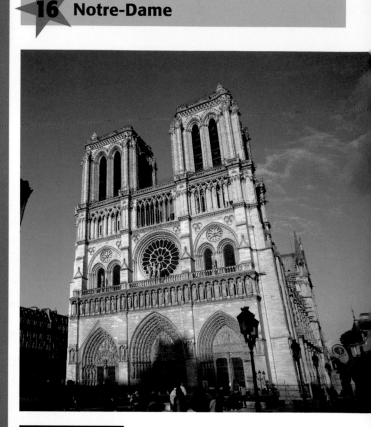

HIGHLIGHTS

- The towers
- Rose windows
- Portals
- Flying buttresses
- The gargoyles
- Emmanuel bell
- Organ
- *Pietà*, Coustou
- Statue of Notre-Dame de Paris (14th-century Virgin and Child)

Spectacular is the word to describe this extraordinary monument, with its world-renowned flying buttresses. There are fine views of the cathedral to be had all over the city, including from the river.

Evolution Construction of Notre-Dame started in 1163 and didn't finish until 1345. Since then the cathedral has suffered from pollution, politics, aesthetic trends and religious change. Most of the stained-glass windows were replaced with clear glass (the stained glass was later restored) in the 18th century, when Revolutionary zeal tore down statues and the spire was dismantled. Not least, Viollet-le-Duc, the fervent 19th-century medievalist architect, was let loose on its restoration and initiated radical alterations.

From far left: The awe-inspiring Notre-Dame, which was badly damaged in a fire in 2019; stained-glass windows in the cathedral's Chapelle Saint-Georges; statue of the Virgin and Child

Interior grandeur The hushed, softly lit stone interior contains numerous chapels, tombs and statues. The sacristy on the south side of the choir is where the treasures of Notre-Dame are usually kept. The magnificent stained glass above the mighty organ is one of the largest in Europe. Walk round the outside of the cathedral for a view of its extravagant flying buttresses and iconic towers.

Destruction In April 2019, a fire broke out in a section of the cathedral that was undergoing renovations. The wooden interior was destroyed, which brought down the 93m (305ft) spire and roof, though the stone towers and many of the treasures appear to have been saved. The extent of the damage means at least five years of renovation work lie ahead.

THE BASICS

notredamedeparis.fr
tours-notre-dame-de-paris
✚ J7
✉ Place du Parvis Notre-Dame–Place Jean-Paul II, 75004
☎ 01 42 34 56 10; Crypt 01 55 42 50 10
🕐 Check online for opening times and advice for visitors following the fire
🚇 Cité, Saint-Michel
🚌 21, 38, 47, 58, 70, 75, 96
🚆 RER Lines B and C, Saint-Michel
♿ Good (not in towers)
📋 Cathedral, towers and Crypt not accessible during renovations

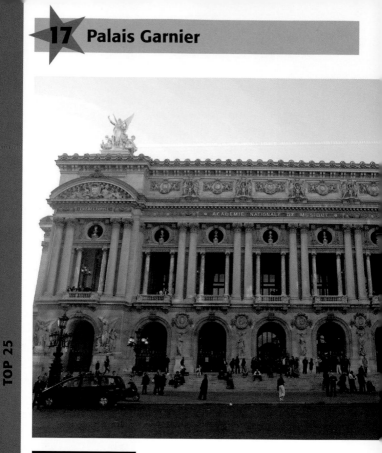

HIGHLIGHTS

- Grand Staircase
- Grand Foyer
- Auditorium
- Facade
- The shop, Galerie de l'Opéra de Paris (▷ 126)

This ornate wedding cake of a building, with sumptuous details decorating its every surface, presents the perfect epitaph to the frenetic architectural activities of France's Second Empire.

Past glory When Charles Garnier's opera house was inaugurated in 1875 it marked the end of Haussmann's ambitious urban face-lift and announced the cultural transition to the Belle Époque, with Nijinsky and Diaghilev's Ballets Russes as later highlights. The opera house, and a fatal accident with a chandelier in 1896, was the inspiration for the novel *The Phantom of the Opera* (1910) by Gaston Leroux. Today, it stages both dance and opera. Rudolf Nureyev was director of the Paris Ballet here between 1983 and 1989.

From left: The ornate façade of the Palais Garnier; one of Carrier-Belleuse's lamp-bearing statues; the gilded statue of Poetry on the roof of the building

Dazzle The Palais Garnier's extravagant, regilded façade of arches, winged horses, friezes, columns and much statuary, topped by a verdigris dome, leads into a majestic foyer. This is dominated by the Grand Staircase, dripping with balconies and chandeliers, which sweeps up to the Grand Foyer with its gilded mirrors, marble, murals and Murano glass. Don't miss the equally ornate auditorium, with its dazzling gold-leaf decorations and red-velvet seats, and Marc Chagall's incongruous and, at the time of its installation in 1964, controversial modernist ceiling whose naive scenes pay tribute to great opera and ballet and include recognizable Paris monuments. The auditorium can be visited except during rehearsals. The opera house also has a library and a museum of operatic memorabilia.

THE BASICS

operadeparis.fr

✚ G3

✉ Place de l'Opéra, 75009

☎ 0892 89 90 90 (35¢ per minute)

🕐 Daily 10–4.30; ticket office Mon–Sat 11.30–6.30 (also one hour before performances)

🍴 Restaurant, bar

Ⓜ Opéra

🚌 20, 21, 27, 29, 32, 45, 52, 66, 68, 95

🚆 RER Line A, Auber

♿ Few; tel 01 40 01 18 50

💰 Moderate

❓ Guided tours in English daily 11am and 2.30pm (expensive). Audio guide in English

47

HIGHLIGHTS

- Oscar Wilde's tomb
- Edith Piaf's tomb
- Chopin's tomb
- Marcel Proust's tomb
- Mur des Fédérés
- Delacroix's tomb
- Baron Haussmann's tomb
- Molière's tomb
- Jim Morrison's tomb

TIP

Beware "unofficial" guides loitering by cemetery gates. Book tours through the official website.

If you think cemeteries are somber places then a visit here may change your mind. The plethora of tomb designs, trees and twisting paths creates a tranquil setting.

Pilgrimage This landscaped hillside, east of the city center, is a popular haunt for rock fans, Piaf fans and lovers of poetry, literature, music and history. Since its creation in 1804 this vast cemetery has seen hundreds of famous people buried within its precincts, so that a walk around its labyrinthine expanse presents a microcosm of French socio-cultural history. Pick up a map at the entrance or plot your visit in advance on the website.

Tombs and graves The cemetery was created in 1804 on Jesuit land where Louis XIV's

Clockwise from far left: Laid out in 1804 on the slopes of a hill in Ménilmontant, the cemetery is pleasantly shaded by trees; you can find peace and solitude at Père Lachaise; one of the many poignant statues; huge monuments line the wide avenues of the cemetery

confessor, Father La Chaise, once lived. It was the site of the Communards' tragic last stand in 1871, when the 147 survivors of a night-long fight met their bloody end in front of a government firing squad and were thrown into a communal grave, now commemorated by the Mur des Fédérés in the eastern corner. Memorials also commemorate victims of the Nazi concentration camps. Paths meander past striking funerary monuments and the graves of such well-known people as the star-crossed medieval lovers Abélard and Héloïse, painters Delacroix and Modigliani, actress Sarah Bernhardt, composers Poulenc and Bizet, and writers Balzac and Colette. Crowds of rock fans throng the tomb of Jim Morrison, singer with The Doors, who died in Paris in 1971.

THE BASICS

paris.fr/cimetieres

➕ See map ▷ 115

✉ Boulevard de Ménilmontant/rue du Repos, 75020

☎ 01 55 25 82 10

🕐 Mid-Mar to early Nov Mon–Fri 8–6, Sat 8.30–6, Sun 9–6; early Nov to mid-Mar Mon–Fri 8–5.30, Sat 8.30–5.30, Sun 9–5.30

🚇 Père Lachaise, Philippe Auguste, Gambetta

🚌 61, 69

♿ Few

💶 Free; tours moderate

❓ The Paris Tourist Office (parisinfo.com) has a list of guides offering tours of the cemetery

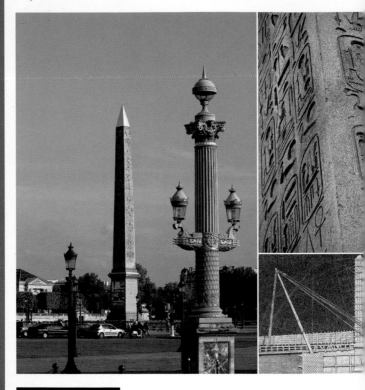

HIGHLIGHTS

● Jeu de Paume
● Musée de l'Orangerie
(▷ 71–72)
● Hôtel de Crillon
● *Chevaux de Marly*
(reproductions)
● View up the
Champs-Élysées

As you stand in this noisy, traffic-choked square, it is hard to imagine the crowds baying for the deaths of Louis XVI and Marie-Antoinette, who were both guillotined here at the height of the French Revolution.

Gruesome history This pulsating square was initially laid out in the mid-18th century to accommodate a statue of King Louis XV. Under the new name of place de la Révolution, it then witnessed mass executions during the French Revolution and was finally renamed the place de la Concorde in 1795, as revolutionary zeal abated. In the same year, Guillaume Coustou's *Chevaux de Marly* were erected at the base of the Champs-Élysées (today reproductions; the originals are in the Louvre). Crowning the

Clockwise from far left: The ancient Egyptian obelisk takes pride of place; hieroglyphs on the obelisk; detail on a fountain; fountains play in elaborate splendor on the place de la Concorde; statues beneath the fountain; a diagram showing the erection of the obelisk

middle of the Concorde is a 3,000-year-old Egyptian obelisk overlooking eight symbolic statues of French cities. Use the pedestrian crossing to reach the central island for a closer look at the obelisk, framed by two fountains.

Grandeur To the north, on either side of the rue Royale, stand the colonnaded Hôtel de Crillon, one of the finest hotels in the city (on the left), and the matching Hôtel de la Marine (right), home to France's Naval staff, both pre-Revolutionary relics. The rue Royale, with its luxury establishments, leads to the Madeleine. The eastern side of the Concorde is dominated by two public art galleries, both in the Jardin des Tuileries (▷ 26–27). The Jeu de Paume focuses on photography, while nearer the river is the beautifully renovated Orangerie (▷ 71–72).

THE BASICS

🔠 E4–F4

✉ Place de la Concorde, 75008

☎ Jeu de Paume 01 47 03 12 50, jeudepaume.org

🕐 Jeu de Paume Tue 11–9, Wed–Sun 11–7

Ⓜ Concorde

🚌 42, 45, 72, 73, 84, 94

♿ Jeu de Paume inexpensive

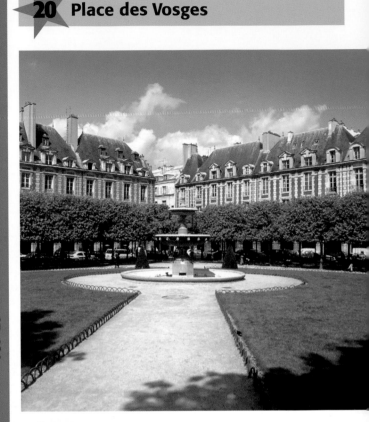

HIGHLIGHTS

- Pavillon du Roi
- Pavillon de la Reine
- Statue of Louis XIII
- No. 6, Maison de Victor Hugo
- No. 21, residence of Cardinal Richelieu
- Door knockers
- Trompe-l'œil bricks
- Four matching fountains

Paris's oldest and best-preserved square connects the quarters of the Marais and the Bastille. You can marvel at its architectural unity and stroll under the arcades, now animated by outdoor restaurants and window-shoppers.

Place Royale Ever since the square was inaugurated in 1612 with a fireworks display, countless luminaries have chosen to live in the redbrick houses overlooking the central garden of plane trees. Before that, the square was the site of a royal palace, the Hôtel des Tournelles (1388), which was abandoned and demolished by Catherine de' Medici in 1559, when her husband Henri II died there. The arcaded facades were commissioned by Henri IV, who incorporated two royal pavilions at the

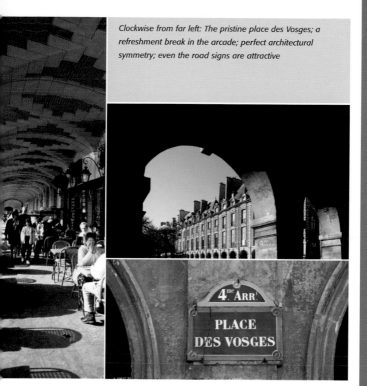

Clockwise from far left: The pristine place des Vosges; a refreshment break in the arcade; perfect architectural symmetry; even the road signs are attractive

4ᵐᵉ ARR.

PLACE DES VOSGES

heart of the north and south sides of the square and named it place Royale.

Exclusive address After the Revolution the square was renamed place des Vosges in tribute to the first French district to pay its new taxes. The first example of planned development in the city, these 36 town houses, with their steep-pitched roofs, surround a formal garden laid out with gravel paths and fountains, all beautifully symmetrical. The square has attracted many famous residents, including princesses, official mistresses, Cardinal Richelieu, Victor Hugo (his house is now a museum) and Théophile Gautier. Smart shops and chic art galleries, with prices to match, line the square's arcades and are ideal for window-shopping.

THE BASICS

paris.fr

➕ M6

✉ Place des Vosges, 75004

🎭 Maison Victor Hugo Tue–Sun 10–6

🍴 Several

🚇 Bastille, Chemin Vert, Saint-Paul

🚌 29, 69, 76

♿ Good

🎟 Free

HIGHLIGHTS

- La Savoyarde bell
- View from the dome
- Mosaic of Christ
- Treasure of Sacré-Cœur
- Bronze doors at Saint-Pierre
- Stained glass
- Statue of Christ
- Statue of the Virgin Mary and Child
- The funicular ride from place Saint-Pierre
- Hearing the choir sing during a service

TIP

- Sacré-Cœur is a pleasant 10-minute walk from Abbesses or Anvers Métro. Or take the Montmartrobus from Abbesses to place du Tertre, from where it's a short walk.

Few people would admit it, but the high point of a trip here is not the basilica itself but the stunning views. You can't forget, however, that Sacré-Cœur was built in memory of the 58,000 dead of the Franco-Prussian War.

Perpetual prayer Although construction started in 1875, it wasn't until 1914 that this white neo-Romanesque-Byzantine edifice was completed, partly due to the problems of laying foundations in the quarry-riddled hill of Montmartre. Priests still work in relays to maintain the tradition of perpetual prayer for forgiveness for the horrors of war and atonement for those slaughtered during the Franco-Prussian war of 1870–71 and, also in 1871, the massacre of some 20,000

Clockwise from far left: Walking up to Sacré-Cœur; equestrian statue of Joan of Arc by Hippolyte Lefèbvre; mosaic of Christ in the basilica; one of the best views in Paris

Communards by government troops. The square bell tower was an afterthought and houses one of the world's heaviest bells, La Savoyarde, which weighs in at 19 tons. The stained-glass windows are replacements of those shattered in WWII.

Panoramas This unmistakable feature of the Paris skyline magnetizes the crowds arriving by funicular or via the steep steps of the terraced garden. For the best views, dawn and dusk offer particularly sparkling panoramas over the city, especially from the exterior terrace of the dome, the second-highest point in Paris after the Eiffel Tower. To the west of Sacré-Cœur is the diminutive Saint-Pierre, a charming church and all that remains of the Benedictine abbey of Montmartre consecrated in 1147.

sacre-coeur-montmartre. com

➕ c1

✉ Parvis du Sacré-Cœur, 75018

☎ 01 53 41 89 00

🕐 Daily 6am–10.30pm; dome and crypt 9.30–8 (5 in winter)

🚇 Abbesses (from here, walk along rue Yvonne Le Tac and rue Tardieu, then take funicular or walk up steps) or Anvers

🚌 Montmartrobus, 30, 40, 54, 85

♿ Wheelchair access from back of basilica

🎫 Basilica free; dome moderate

HIGHLIGHTS

- Rose window
- Oratory
- Tombs of canons
- Stained-glass depiction of Christ's Passion
- Saint Louis in the "Story of the Relics" window

TIPS

- The upper chapel can become extremely crowded. The quietest times to visit are Tuesday and Friday morning.
- Lines for tickets can be long so buy a ticket at La Conciergerie (▷ 18) if you want to save time.

Sainte-Chapelle's spire, towering 75m (246ft) above the ground, is in itself a great expression of faith, but this is surpassed inside by the glowing intensity of the stained-glass windows climbing to a star-studded roof, now spectacularly restored.

A masterpiece One of Paris's oldest and most significant monuments stands in the precincts of the Palais de Justice. The chapel was built by Louis IX (later canonized) to house the relics he had acquired at exorbitant cost during the crusades, including what was reputed to be the Crown of Thorns, and fragments of the Cross and drops of Christ's blood (now kept with the treasures of Notre-Dame). Pierre de Montreuil is believed to have masterminded this delicate Gothic construction, bypassing the

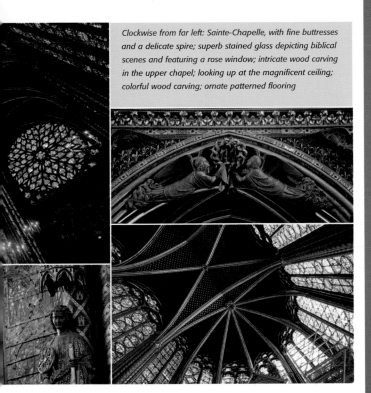

Clockwise from far left: Sainte-Chapelle, with fine buttresses and a delicate spire; superb stained glass depicting biblical scenes and featuring a rose window; intricate wood carving in the upper chapel; looking up at the magnificent ceiling; colorful wood carving; ornate patterned flooring

need for flying buttresses, incorporating a lower chapel for palace servants and installing more than 600 sq m (6,458 sq ft) of striking stained glass above. Completed in 1248 in record time, it was Louis IX's private chapel, with discreet access from what was then the royal palace.

Apocalypse More than 1,000 biblical scenes are illustrated in 15 windows, starting with Genesis to the left of the entrance, and working round the chapel to finish with the Apocalypse, in the rose window. The only non-biblical theme is in the 16th window, which tells how the holy relics came to Paris. Two-thirds of the windows are 13th-century originals—the oldest stained glass in Paris. The statues of the Apostles are copies; the originals are at the Musée de Cluny —Musée national du Moyen-Âge (▷ 30–31).

THE BASICS

sainte-chapelle.fr

➕ J6

✉ 8 boulevard du Palais, Île de la Cité, 75001

☎ 01 53 40 60 80

🕐 Apr–Sep daily 9–7; Oct–Mar daily 9–5

🚇 Cité, Châtelet

🚌 21, 27, 38, 53, 85, 96

🚆 RER Line B, Saint-Michel

♿ Moderate (joint ticket expensive, ▷ panel 56)

❓ Guided tours in English; call for times

★23 Seine Boat Trip

THE BOAT TRIP

Distance: 11km (7 miles)
Allow: Just over 1 hour
Start/End: Square du Vert-Galant, Pont Neuf
How to get there:
🚇 Pont Neuf
🚌 27, 58, 63, 70, 84, 86, 89, 96
From the Métro station, walk over the Pont Neuf. About halfway across, on the right, is a sign for the Vedettes du Pont Neuf. Go down the steps to the square.

TIPS

● Evening, when the monuments are lit up, is a great time to go on this trip.
● A more flexible way to enjoy the river is the hop-on, hop-off Batobus shuttle service (▷ 167).

A pleasant river cruise along the Seine is a great way to view some of Paris's key sights from a different perspective. And in just over an hour you can see many of the famous landmarks.

Romantic trip The boat leaves from square du Vert-Galant and heads west. On the Right Bank you can see the Museé du Louvre (▷ 32–33). After passing under the Pont du Carrousel and the Pont Royal you'll see the Musée d'Orsay (▷ 38–39) on the Left Bank and then the 18th-century Palais Bourbon. On the Right Bank is place de la Concorde (▷ 50–51). The boat passes under the ornate Pont Alexandre III (▷ 74). On the Right Bank are the Grand Palais and Petit Palais (▷ 68) and on the Left Bank, in the distance, is Les Invalides (▷ 22–23).

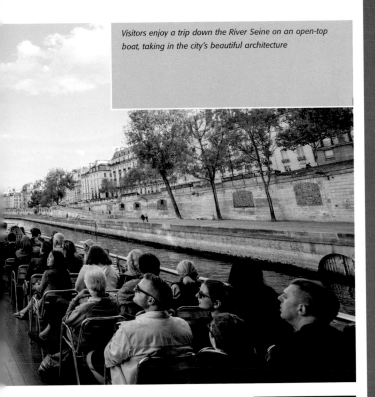

Visitors enjoy a trip down the River Seine on an open-top boat, taking in the city's beautiful architecture

After passing under the Pont des Invalides, the Pont de l'Alma and the Passerelle Debilly, the boat rounds a bend to unveil a spectacular view of the Eiffel Tower (▷ 60–61) on the Left Bank. It then passes under the Pont d'Iéna, which spans the river between the Eiffel Tower and the Jardins du Trocadéro, before turning and heading back in the opposite direction to the Île de la Cité. You'll see the cupola of the Institut de France on the right before you pass under the southern side of the Pont Neuf. The next two bridges are the Pont Saint-Michel, leading to the Latin Quarter and the Sorbonne university, and the Petit Pont, the smallest bridge in Paris. On the Île de la Cité you can see Notre-Dame cathedral (▷ 44–45); the boat then circles the picturesque Île Saint-Louis before returning to the Pont Neuf past the Conciergerie.

THE BASICS

vedettesdupontneuf.com
☎ 01 46 33 98 38
🕐 Check online for sailing times
💶 Moderate
❓ Tours in English and French. Pick up a free route map from the boarding platform. Other options: Bateaux Parisiens (bateauxparisiens.com, tel 08 25 01 01 01) and Compagnie des Bateaux Mouches (bateaux-mouches.fr, tel 01 42 25 96 10)

HIGHLIGHTS

- Panoramic views
- Gustave Eiffel's office
- Sparkling lights
- Glass floor at level 1

TIPS

- To skip the wait for the elevators, walk up the stairs to level two, then catch the elevator to the top. The climb isn't too daunting. Alternatively, buy your tickets online.
- The wait for the elevator is generally shorter at night.
- Strollers (buggies) are allowed up the tower only if they are collapsible.

The Eiffel Tower could be a cliché but it isn't. The powerful silhouette of Gustave Eiffel's marvel of engineering still makes a stirring sight, especially at night when its delicate, lace-like iron structure is accentuated by lights.

Glittering feat Built in a record two years for the 1889 Exposition Universelle, the Eiffel Tower was never intended to be a permanent feature of the city. However, in 1910 it was finally saved for posterity, preparing the way for today's 6.7 million annual visitors. Avoid a long wait for the elevator by visiting the tower at night, when it fully lives up to its romantic image and provides a glittering spectacle, whether of the illuminated tower itself or of the carpet of nocturnal Paris unfolding at its feet.

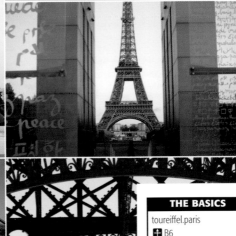

Clockwise from far left: The icon of Paris, set in the Champ de Mars; view of the tower from the Jardins du Trocadéro; the tower framed by the Wall of Peace; detail of the lace-like iron structure; the lower section dwarfs the crowds

More than 330 spotlights illuminate the iron latticework, topped by a rotating beacon. After dusk the tower sparkles for 5 minutes every hour on the hour until 1am, thanks to 20,000 randomly flashing low-energy bulbs.

Violent reactions Gustave Eiffel was a master of cast-iron structures. His 324m (1,063ft) tower attracted great opposition, but his genius was vindicated by the fact that it sways no more than 9cm (3.5in) in high winds and remained the world's highest structure for 40 years. Eiffel kept an office here until his death in 1923; at the top, there is a re-creation of Thomas Edison's visit on 10 September 1889. A 3m- (10ft-)high glass screen now surrounds the base of the tower, increasing site security yet allowing a full view of the city icon.

THE BASICS

toureiffel.paris

✚ B6

✉ Quai Branly, Champ de Mars, 75007

☎ 08 25 56 66 62; from outside France 01 76 64 14 64

🕐 Daily 9.30am–11.45pm; last elevator up at 10.30pm (stairs 9.30–6.30)

🍽 Le 58 (1st floor, 08 25 56 66 62); Le Jules Verne (2nd floor, ▷ 149)

🚇 Bir-Hakeim, Trocadéro

🚌 30, 42, 69, 82, 86, 92

🚆 RER Line C, Tour Eiffel

♿ Very good (to 2nd floor). Wheelchair users are unable to go to the very top

💰 Expensive; stairs moderate

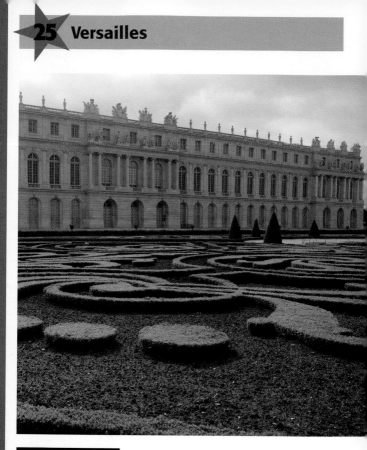

HIGHLIGHTS

- Hall of Mirrors
- Petit Trianon
- Formal gardens
- Grandes Eaux
- Hameau and farm
- Buffet d'Eau, Grand Trianon
- Opera house

TIP

- Attend a performance to see the interior of the splendid 18th-century royal opera house.

The Château de Versailles has undergone a massive renovation that has restored much of the grandeur enjoyed by the Sun King, Louis XIV, who commissioned the palace.

A new palace Versailles is the ultimate symbol of French grandeur, and the backdrop to the end of the monarchy in 1789. Louis XIV moved his court to the site of his father's hunting lodge, creating a royal residence, seat of government and home to French nobility. Building continued until his death in 1715, by which time the 100ha (247-acre) garden had been perfected by landscape garden designer André Le Nôtre.

Glorious gardens With their geometric beds, vast watercourses and splendid fountains

Clockwise from far left: The magnificent château and the elaborate formal gardens; the lawns and lake with the Latona fountain in the foreground; the delightful floral fountain; ceiling detail in the Hall of Mirrors; the stunning Hall of Mirrors, the central feature of the château

THE BASICS

chateauversailles.fr

✚ See map ▷ 114

✉ Place d'Armes, Versailles, 78000

☎ 01 30 83 78 00

🕐 State apartments: Apr–Oct Tue–Sun 9–6.30; Nov–Mar Tue–Sun 9–5.30. Grand and Petit Trianon: Tue–Sun 12–5.30 (until 6.30 in summer). Park: daily 8am–8.30pm (8–6 in winter). Fountains: Apr–Oct Sat–Sun 11–12, 3.30–5 (also late May–late Jun Tue 11–12, 2.30–4)

🚆 RER C, Versailles Rive Gauche

♿ Few (state apartments)

🎟 Passport ticket (1- or 2-day) for all palaces expensive (visitors with disabilities free); park free; Grandes Eaux and Jardins Musicaux moderate Apr–Oct. (If you have tickets, go to the A access. If not, go to Ticket Information, South Ministers' Wing.) Free first Sun of month Nov–Mar

❓ Guided tours

(flowing weekends Apr–Oct), the palace gardens are the perfect expression of the formal French style. Geometry rules, too, in the floral gardens at the lavish royal retreat of Grand Trianon, but Marie-Antoinette's romantic estate at the Petit Trianon is informal and pretty. It comprises a small château, belvedere, a rustic hamlet (Hameau de la Reine) and the notorious but delightful farm where the queen liked to play at being a milkmaid.

Architectural highlights The magnificence of the Hall of Mirrors is the highlight of the Grands Appartements, where you can also access the opulent Queen's Chamber (closed for renovation). At weekends, you can visit the more intimate apartments of the Dauphin and Louis XV's daughters.

More to See

This section contains other great places to visit if you have more time. Some are in the heart of the city while others are a short journey away, found under Farther Afield. This chapter also has fantastic excursions that you should set aside a whole day to visit.

In the Heart of the City

CAFÉ BEAUBOURG

cafebeaubourg.com

Opposite the Pompidou Centre, this café is frequented by artists, critics and book-reading poseurs.

🚇 K5 💺 43 rue Saint-Merri, 75004 ☎ 01 48 87 63 96 ⏰ Daily 8am–2am. Last orders midnight 🚇 Hôtel de Ville, Châtelet, Rambuteau

CAFÉ LES DEUX MAGOTS

lesdeuxmagots.fr

This famous Left Bank café attracts a mix of tourists and those following in the footsteps of Albert Camus and Ernest Hemingway.

🚇 G6 💺 6 place Saint-Germain-des-Prés, 75006 ☎ 01 45 48 55 25 ⏰ Daily 7.30am–1am 🚇 Saint-Germain-des-Prés

CAFÉ DE FLORE

Cafedeflore.fr

Haunted by ghosts of existentialists Sartre and de Beauvoir, who held court here during the German Occupation, this café is pricey but a good spot for people-watching.

🚇 G6 💺 172 boulevard Saint-Germain, 75006 ☎ 01 45 48 55 26 ⏰ Daily 7.30am–1.30am 🚇 Saint-Germain-des-Prés

CATACOMBES DE PARIS

catacombes.paris.fr

Go underground to learn more about the hidden history of Paris. Parisians exploited the geology in medieval times when they dug huge subterranean quarries for the stone that built the city. In 1786 it was consecrated as the site of the Paris Municipal Ossuary. A 1.5km (1-mile) one-way route leads through the huge vaults lined with human bones transferred from the city cemeteries. The catacombs are 20m (66ft) below ground and there are 131 steps down, with 112 steps back to street level.

🚇 Off map at F9 💺 1 avenue du Colonel Henri Rol-Tanguy (place Denfert-Rochereau), 75014 ☎ 01 43 22 47 63 ⏰ Tue–Sun 10–8.30 🚇 Denfert-Rochereau

CIMETIÈRE DE MONTMARTRE

Montmartre's cemetery has many graves of the famous, including writers Henri Stendhal and Alexandre Dumas, and artists Edgar Degas and Jean-Baptiste Greuze. The tomb of Émile Zola is near the main entrance, although

Outside Café les Deux Magots

Monument at the Cimetière de Montmartre

the writer's remains were moved to the Panthéon in 1908.

➕ a1 ✉ 20 avenue Rachel, 75018
☎ 01 53 42 36 30 🕐 Mid-Mar to early Nov Mon–Fri 8–6, Sat 8.30–6, Sun 9–6; early Nov to mid-Mar Mon–Sat 8–5.30, Sun 9–5.30. Last entry 15 mins before closing 🚇 Place de Clichy, Blanche

DOMAINE NATIONAL DU PALAIS-ROYAL

domaine-palais-royal.fr

Elegant 18th-century shopping arcades surround this garden and palace (now the Conseil Constitutionnel and the Ministère de la Culture). Daniel Buren's striking striped columns occupy the Cour d'Honneur.

➕ H4 ✉ Place du Palais-Royal, 75001
☎ 01 47 03 92 16 🕐 Daily Jun–Aug 7am–11pm; Apr–May 7am–10.15pm; Sep 7am–9.30pm; Oct–Mar 7.30am–8.30pm
🍴 Plenty 🚇 Palais-Royal–Musée du Louvre

ÉGLISE SAINT-ÉTIENNE-DU-MONT

saintetiennedumont.fr

Dating from the 15th century, this church has a combination of Gothic, Renaissance and classical architecture. The unique screen arching over the nave is a highlight.

➕ J8 ✉ Place Sainte-Geneviève, 75005
☎ 01 43 54 11 79 🕐 Mon 2.30–7.30, Tue–Fri 8.30–7.30, Sat–Sun 8.30–1 and 2–8
🚇 Cardinal Lemoine

ÉGLISE SAINT-EUSTACHE

saint-eustache.org

Renaissance in decoration and detail but Gothic in general design, this church has frequent organ recitals by well-known players.

➕ J4–5 ✉ 2 impasse Saint-Eustache, 75001 ☎ 01 42 36 31 05 🕐 Mon–Fri 9.30–7, Sat 10–7.15, Sun 9–7.15 🚇 Les Halles

ÉGLISE SAINT-GERMAIN-DES-PRÉS

eglise-saintgermaindespres.fr

Paris's oldest church dates from the 11th century and preserves an original tower and choir. There are organ and concert recitals.

➕ G6 ✉ Place Saint-Germain-des-Prés, 75006 ☎ 01 55 42 81 18 🕐 Sun–Mon 9am–8pm, Tue–Sat 8.30am–8pm
🚇 Saint-Germain-des-Prés

Église Saint-Eustache

Église Saint-Germain-des-Prés

ÉGLISE SAINT-MERRI

saintmerry.org

This superb example of Flamboyant Gothic, not completed until 1612, has Renaissance stained glass, murals and an impressive organ loft. It also holds concerts.

➕ J5/K5 ✉ 76 rue de la Verrerie, 75004 ☎ 01 42 71 93 93 🕐 Apr–Oct daily 3–7; Nov–Mar 2–6. See accueilmusical.fr for concert information Ⓜ Hôtel de Ville

ÉGLISE SAINT-SÉVERIN

saint-severin.com

Built between the 13th and 16th centuries on the site of an 11th-century church, the church features lovely stained glass and palm-tree vaulting.

➕ J7 ✉ 3 rue des Prêtres Saint-Séverin, 75005 ☎ 01 42 34 93 50 🕐 Mon–Sat 11–7.30, Sun 9–8.30 Ⓜ Saint-Michel, Cluny–La Sorbonne

ÉGLISE SAINT-SULPICE

Work started here in 1646, ending 134 years later with asymmetrical towers and mixed styles. Note Delacroix's murals in the first chapel on the right.

➕ G7 ✉ Place Saint-Sulpice, 75006 ☎ 01 42 34 59 94 🕐 Daily 7.30–7.30 Ⓜ Saint-Sulpice

GRAND PALAIS AND PETIT PALAIS

grandpalais.fr
petitpalais.paris.fr

These two fine buildings were erected for the Universal Exposition of 1900 in the beaux-arts style. Today the Petit Palais houses a permanent collection as the Musée des Beaux-Arts, with pieces from the Classical era to the early 20th century. The Grand Palais will be closed from 2020 to 2023 for renovations.

➕ D4/E4 ✉ Grand Palais: avenue du General Eisenhower. Petit Palais: avenue Winston Churchill ☎ Grand Palais: 01 44 13 17 17. Petit Palais: 01 53 43 40 00 Ⓜ Champs-Élysées–Clemenceau

ÎLE SAINT-LOUIS

An oasis of calm, the Île Saint-Louis maintains a spirit of its own. Rue Saint-Louis-en-l'Île is lined with art shops and restaurants.

➕ K7 Ⓜ Pont Marie, Sully Morland

Vaulted ceiling, Gothic arches and stained glass inside Église Saint-Séverin

INSTITUT DU MONDE ARABE

imarabe.org

The high-tech reinterpretation of traditional Arab fretwork is the hallmark here. The museum has fine metalwork, ceramics, textiles, carpets and calligraphy.

🚩 K7 ✉ 1 rue des Fossés Saint-Bernard, 75005 ☎ 01 40 51 38 38 🕐 Tue–Fri 10–6, Sat–Sun 10–7 🚇 Cardinal Lemoine, Jussieu 💶 Moderate

MAISON EUROPÉENNE DE LA PHOTOGRAPHIE

mep-fr.org

This is a stylish complex for contemporary photography, with dynamic temporary shows. The galleries are spread over five floors.

🚩 L6 ✉ 5–7 rue de Fourcy, 75004 ☎ 01 44 78 75 00 🕐 Wed, Fri 11–8, Thu 11–10, Sat–Sun 10–8 🚇 Saint-Paul 💶 Moderate

MÉMORIAL DE LA SHOAH

memorialdelashoah.org

This moving Holocaust museum contains a wall inscribed with the names of the 76,000 Jewish people deported from France between 1942 and 1944. It also mounts temporary exhibitions on Holocaust-related themes.

🚩 K6 ✉ 17 rue Geoffroy-l'Asnier, 75004 ☎ 01 42 77 44 72 🕐 Sun–Fri 10–6 (Thu until 10) 🚇 Saint-Paul, Hôtel de Ville, Pont Marie 💶 Free

MUSÉE D'ART ET D'HISTOIRE DU JUDAÏSME

mahj.org

Jewish art and culture are on display here, from medieval times to the present day, from France, the rest of Europe and North Africa. Exhibits range from wedding items, *objets d'art*, manuscripts and textiles to the work of artists such as Modigliani and Chagall.

🚩 K5 ✉ Hôtel de Saint-Aignan, 71 rue du Temple, 75003 ☎ 01 53 01 86 60 🕐 Mon–Fri 11–6, Sat–Sun 10–6. Last admission 45 mins before closing 🚇 Rambuteau, Hôtel de Ville 💶 Moderate

MUSÉE D'ART MODERNE DE LA VILLE DE PARIS

mam.paris.fr

The galleries benefited from an extensive renovation program completed in 2019. The collection

A sign at the Maison Européenne de la Photographie

Musée d'Art et d'Histoire du Judaïsme

here covers fauvism, cubism, surrealism, abstract and nouveau réalisme. The museum occupies the east wing of the Palais de Tokyo; the west wing houses the Centre d'Art Contemporain.

➕ B4 ✉ 11 avenue du Président Wilson, 75016 ☎ 01 53 67 40 00 🕐 Tue–Wed, Fri–Sun 10–6, Thu 10–10. Last admission 45 mins before closing 🚇 Iéna, Alma–Marceau 🎫 Free; temporary exhibitions moderate

MUSÉE DES ARTS DÉCORATIFS
lesartsdecoratifs.fr

This collection of decorative arts is enriched by contributions from 20th-century designers such as Le Corbusier, Mallet-Stevens, Niki de Saint Phalle and Philippe Starck. Another branch of the museum is the Musée Nissim Camondo on rue de Monceau, an early 20th-century mansion complete with original decor.

➕ G5 ✉ 107 rue de Rivoli, 75001 ☎ 01 44 55 57 50 🕐 Tue–Sun 11–6 (Thu until 9). Last admission 30 mins before closing 🚇 Palais-Royal–Musée du Louvre 🎫 Moderate; combined ticket expensive

MUSÉE DES ARTS ET MÉTIERS
arts-et-metiers.net

Art meets science at this museum through antique clocks, optics, underwater items including a diving suit, vintage cars and mechanical toys.

➕ K4 ✉ 60 rue Réaumur, 75003 ☎ 01 53 01 82 75 🕐 Tue–Sun 10–6 (Thu until 9.30pm) 🚇 Arts et Métiers, Réaumur–Sébastopol 🎫 Inexpensive

MUSÉE CARNAVALET
carnavalet.paris.fr

Renovations to this major museum, dedicated to the long history of Paris, have improved access to its 615,000 artifacts.

➕ L6 ✉ 23 rue Sévigné, 75003 ☎ 01 44 59 58 58 🚇 Saint-Paul 🚌 29, 69, 76, 96

MUSÉE COGNACQ-JAY
museecognacqjay.paris.fr

In a magnificent Marais mansion furnished in 18th-century style, you can see the 18th-century paintings and *objets d'art* collected by Ernest Cognacq and his wife Louise Jay, founders of the La Samaritaine department store.

Musée d'Art Moderne de la Ville de Paris

Modern design at the Musée des Arts Décoratifs

L6 ⊠ Hôtel Donon, 8 rue Elzévir, 75003
☎ 01 40 27 07 21 🕐 Tue–Sun 10–6
🚇 Saint-Paul 🎟 Free

MUSÉE GUSTAVE MOREAU
musee-moreau.fr

This studio-museum, on the edge of Pigalle, presents an intriguing view of how a late-19th-century artist lived and worked. On the second and third floors are the studios of the symbolist painter Gustave Moreau (1826–98), teacher to Henri Matisse; on the first floor is a reconstruction of Moreau's private apartment.

G2 ⊠ 14 rue de la Rochefoucauld, 75009 ☎ 01 48 74 38 50 🕐 Wed–Mon 10–6 🚇 Trinité 🎟 Inexpensive; free first Sun of the month

MUSÉE JACQUEMART-ANDRÉ
musee-jacquemart-andre.com

This elegant mansion was built between 1869 and 1876 for the Parisian financier Eduard André and his wife, the artist Nélie Jacquemart. It is filled with original furniture and a fine collection of paintings, including works by Botticelli, Rembrandt, Bellini, Van Dyck, Fragonard and Jacques-Louis David.

D2 ⊠ 158 boulevard Haussmann, 75008 ☎ 01 45 62 11 59 🕐 Daily 10–6 🚇 Saint-Philippe-du-Roule, Miromesnil 🎟 Moderate (audio guide inexpensive)

MUSÉE DE MONTMARTRE
museedemontmartre.fr

Montmartre's history includes a headless saint, windmills and a notoriously liberal nightlife. Find out more at the Musée de Montmartre, where you'll find artworks by Toulouse-Lautrec and Modigliani, and the studio of mother and son artists Suzanne Valadon and Maurice Utrillo.

c1 ⊠ 12 rue Cortot, 75018
☎ 01 49 25 89 39 🕐 Apr–Sep daily 10–7; Oct–Mar 10–6 🚇 Lamarck Caulaincourt, Anvers 🎟 Moderate

MUSÉE DE L'ORANGERIE
musee-orangerie.fr

A major repository of 20th-century art, the Orangerie is most famous for Claude Monet's *Water Lilies*, a cycle of paintings donated by the artist in 1918. Almost 100m

Paintings at the Musée Gustave Moreau

(300ft) long, this eight-canvas wonder is a pivotal work of the Impressionist movement.

➕ F4 ✉ Jardin des Tuileries, place de la Concorde, 75001 ☎ 01 44 77 80 07 🕐 Wed–Mon 9–6. Last admission 5.15pm 🚇 Concorde, Tuileries 💷 Inexpensive

MUSÉE YVES SAINT LAURENT

museeyslparis.com
Opened in 2017, this museum is in the building where Yves Saint Laurent (1936–2008) created his haute-couture collections between 1974 and 2002. A constantly changing display showcases his work, from the original sketches that captured his ideas through to the finished catwalk gowns.

➕ B4 ✉ 5 avenue Marceau, 75116 ☎ 01 44 31 64 00 🕐 Tue–Sun 11–6 (Fri until 9pm). Last entry 45 mins before closing 🚇 Alma, Marceau 💷 Inexpensive

MUSÉUM NATIONAL D'HISTOIRE NATURELLE, JARDIN DES PLANTES

mnhn.fr
Set up in 1635 on the initiative of Louis XIII's physician, the Jardin des Plantes is Paris's botanical garden, complete with an alpine section and hothouses. Around its fringes are the buildings of the Muséum national d'Histoire Naturelle, of which the garden forms part. These include the Galeries de Paléontologie et d'Anatomie Comparée, housing dinosaur skeletons, and the Grande Galerie de l'Évolution, which has a children's gallery devoted to biodiversity.

➕ K9/L9 ✉ 2 rue Buffon, 75005 ☎ 01 40 79 56 01 🕐 Gardens daily 8–sunset; Grand Galerie Wed–Mon 10–6; Zoo Mon–Fri 9.30–6, Sat–Sun 9.30–7.30 🚇 Gare d'Austerlitz, Jussieu 💷 Gardens free, others moderate to expensive

PALAIS DE CHAILLOT

Built for the Paris exhibition of 1937, the curving wings of the Palais de Chaillot house the Musée national de la Marine (closed for renovation until 2021), the Musée de l'Homme, the Cité de l'Architecture et du Patrimoine and the Théatre de Chaillot. The wonderfully wide-terraced Parvis

Aerial view of the Champ de Mars from the Eiffel Tower

des Libertés et des Droits de l'Homme offers fabulous views across the buildings of Paris.

➕ A5 ✉ Place du Trocadéro, 75116 ☎ Homme 01 44 05 72 72, museedelhomme.fr; Marine 01 53 65 69 69, musee-marine.fr 🚇 Trocadéro
🎫 Moderate

PANTHÉON

paris-pantheon.fr

Occupying a hilltop site close to the Sorbonne and the Quartier Latin, Jacques-Germain Soufflot's neoclassical 18th-century structure provides an imposing setting for the tombs of France's greatest citizens, including Voltaire, Dumas, Rousseau and Marie Curie. From April to October, you can ascend the dome as part of a guided tour.

➕ J8 ✉ Place du Panthéon, 75005 ☎ 01 44 32 18 00 🕐 Apr–Sep daily 10–6.30; Oct–Mar 10–6 🚇 Cardinal Lemoine, Maubert–Mutualité
🎫 Inexpensive

PARC DU CHAMP DE MARS

The lawns of the Champ de Mars stretch out in a rectangular design between the Eiffel Tower and the 18th-century École Militaire. The Romans fought the Celtic Parisii tribe here in 52BC—the park's name, Field of Mars, refers to the Roman god of war. It wasn't until 1765 that the site became a parade ground for the École Militaire. The park has hosted national celebrations, parades, international exhibitions and horse races. Today it is popular with all.

➕ B6–C6 ✉ Champ de Mars, 75007 🚇 École Militaire

PAVILLON DE L'ARSENAL

pavillon-arsenal.com

This strikingly designed building houses well-conceived exhibitions on urban Paris past and present, alongside a display on the city's architectural evolution.

➕ L7 ✉ 21 boulevard Morland, 75004 ☎ 01 42 76 33 97 🕐 Tue–Sun 11–7 🚇 Sully Morland 🎫 Free

PLACE DES ABBESSES

Place des Abbesses is less touristy than place du Tertre, farther up the Montmartre hill, so it's a quieter

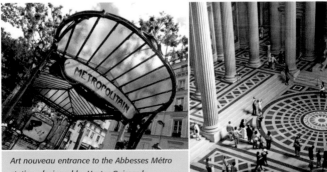

Art nouveau entrance to the Abbesses Métro station, designed by Hector Guimard

The imposing interior of the Panthéon

coffee stop. The magnificent art nouveau Métro entrance here leads into Paris's deepest station, 30m (98.5ft) below ground. It was designed by Hector Guimard (1867–1942) and is one of only three original Guimard entrances left in Paris.

🞢 b2 ✉ Place des Abbesses, Montmartre, 75018 🚇 Abbesses

PONT ALEXANDRE III

Four gilded bronze Pegasus figures watch over this wildly ornate bridge, which forms a link between Les Invalides (▷ 22–23) on the Left Bank and the Grand Palais and Petit Palais (▷ 68) on the Right. Symbolic of the optimism of the Belle Époque, it was built for the 1900 Exposition Universelle.

🞢 D4 ✉ Cours de la Reine/quai d'Orsay 🚇 Invalides, Champs-Élysées–Clémenceau

PONT DE L'ALMA

The first Pont de l'Alma was built in 1856 to commemorate a Franco-British victory in the Crimean War. The bridge was replaced in 1974. The underpass on the Right Bank is the site of the fatal car crash involving Diana, Princess of Wales, in August 1997. The Liberty Flame near the entrance, a symbol of American and French friendship, has become an unofficial memorial to her.

🞢 C4–5 ✉ Place de l'Alma/place de la Résistance 🚇 Alma–Marceau

PONT DES ARTS

The pedestrian bridge of 1804 was replaced in 1984 by an iron structure of seven arches crossed by wooden planks. From the center of the bridge there are excellent views of the Seine.

🞢 H5–6 🚇 Louvre–Rivoli

PONT NEUF

Dating from 1604, Paris's oldest bridge ironically bears the name of New Bridge. The houseless design was highly controversial at the time.

🞢 H6 🚇 Pont Neuf, Île de la Cité

RUE DU CHERCHE-MIDI

César's sculpture on the rue de Sèvres crossroads marks out this typical Left Bank street, home to

Early 17th-century Pont Neuf features 12 stone arches

the famous Poîlane bakery (No. 8) and the Musée Hébert (No. 85).
🗺 G7 🚇 Saint-Sulpice

RUE JACOB
Antiques and interior decoration shops monopolize this picturesque stretch. You can detour to the nearby Musée national Eugène Delacroix on rue de Furstenberg.
🗺 G6 🚇 Saint-Germain-des-Prés

RUE DES ROSIERS
At the heart of Paris's lively Jewish quarter, this effervescent street is packed with synagogues, kosher butchers and restaurants, and Hebrew bookshop, as well as an array of designer boutiques.
🗺 L6 🚇 Saint-Paul

RUE VIEILLE-DU-TEMPLE
The pulse of the hip Marais district, this street is dense with bars, cafés, restaurants and boutiques.
🗺 K6–L5 🚇 Saint-Paul

SQUARE DU VERT-GALANT
Enjoy a quintessential view of the picturesque bridges and the iconic Louvre in this tiny, pretty park, which is also the perfect place for a picnic.
🗺 H6 ✉ Place du Pont-Neuf, 75001 🚇 Pont Neuf

TOUR MONTPARNASSE
tourmontparnasse56.com
When it was constructed in 1973, with its reinforced concrete core, the Tour Montparnasse's 59 floors of smoked glass provoked some indignation. Since then it has become a popular landmark, visible from all over Paris and, from within, its viewing gallery and terrace offer far-reaching views of the city. In mid-2017, plans for a radical redevelopment of the tower were announced. Architects Nouvel AOM will create a "green" facade with terraced gardens which will soften the once controversial and now dated box-like original shape. Tour Montparnasse will reopen to coincide with the summer 2024 Paris Olympics.
🗺 F9 ✉ 33 avenue du Maine, 75015 🚇 Montparnasse–Bienvenüe

César's Centaure, a tribute to Pablo Picasso, on the rue de Sèvres crossroads

Square du Vert-Galant

Farther Afield

FONDATION LOUIS VUITTON
fondationlouisvuitton.fr
Designed by architect Frank Gehry, this superb futuristic edifice hosts a museum that showcases the art collections of the world famous Louis Vuitton French haute-couture house. Regular exhibitions, musical events and family days bring it all to life.
🔳 See map ▷ 114 ✉ 8 avenue du Mahatma Gandhi, Bois de Boulogne, 75116 ☎ 01 40 69 96 00 🕒 Varies according to exhibition. Core hours Mon & Wed–Thu 12–7, Fri–Sun 12–8 🚇 Les Sablons; minibus from place Charles de Gaulle every 15 mins (ticket €2) 💷 Inexpensive

LA GRANDE ARCHE
lagrandearche.fr
This modernist echo of the Arc de Triomphe in white marble and on a grand scale was designed by Johann Otto von Spreckelsen. It's a prominent landmark on the city skyline.
🔳 See map ▷ 114 ✉ 1 parvis de La Défense, 92044 ☎ 01 40 90 52 20 🕒 Daily 10–7 🚇 Grande Arche de La Défense 💷 Expensive

La Grande Arche in La Défense

PARC ANDRÉ-CITROËN
Divided into specialist gardens, this 1990s park lies on the site of a former Citroën factory. You'll find zany experimentation with metal and water, plus a tethered balloon.
🔳 See map ▷ 114 ✉ Rue Cauchy, 75015 🕒 Summer daily 8–dusk (9–dusk rest of year) 🚇 Balard, Javel 💷 Free

PARC DES BUTTES CHAUMONT
The loveliest of Haussmann's parks owes its singular beauty and fine views to its craggy site, a former quarry in the northeast of the city. There is also a children's puppet theater, the Guignol de Paris.
🔳 See map ▷ 115 ✉ 1 rue Botzaris, 75019 🕒 May to mid-Sep daily 7am–10pm; mid- to end Sep 7am–9pm; Oct–Apr 7am–8pm 🚇 Buttes Chaumont 💷 Free

PARC DE LA VILLETTE
lavillette.com
The Parc de la Villette catapults you into a futuristic world. It offers cultural attractions and leisure activities including a science museum, music complex, hemispheric cinema, exhibition venue and the city's flag-ship concert hall, the Philharmonie de Paris, designed by Jean Nouvel. A covered walkway links the Cité des Sciences et de l'Industrie and the Cité de la Musique–Philharmonie de Paris.
🔳 See map ▷ 115 ✉ Park: 211 avenue Jean-Jaurès, 75019 ☎ Park: 01 40 03 75 75. Cité de Sciences et de l'Industrie: 01 40 04 80 00. Cité de la Musique–Philharmonie de Paris: 01 44 84 44 84 🕒 Cité des Sciences et de l'Industrie: Tue–Sat 10–6, Sun 10–7. Cité de la Musique: Tue–Sat 12–6, Sun 10–6 🍴 Cafés, restaurants 🚇 Park: Porte de Pantin. Cité des Sciences et de l'Industrie: Porte de la Villette 💷 Park: free; Cité des Sciences et de l'Industrie: moderate ❓ Reserve activities as soon as you arrive

Excursions

CHANTILLY

domainedechantilly.com

Picturesque Château de Chantilly is surrounded by attractive parkland, with the forest of Chantilly beyond, and contains a magnificent art collection. One of Europe's leading training venues for racehorses, the town of Chantilly is home to a world-famous racecourse and the Musée du Cheval, housed within the Grandes Écuries—a superb 18th-century stable block.

For five centuries, the domain of Chantilly passed from one branch of the same family to another without ever being sold, starting with the Orgemont family in the 14th and 15th centuries before passing to the Montmorency dynasty, one of France's most powerful families. Chantilly passed in turn to the Bourbon Condés, cousins of the kings of France.

The old château was ruined during the Revolution, but in the late 19th century a splendid reconstruction was commissioned by Henri d'Orléans, Duc d'Aumale, the son of King Louis Philippe, who needed somewhere to house his art collection. This still hangs in the Galerie des Peintures in the manner stipulated by him when he bequeathed Chantilly to the nation. The collection includes works by Raphael and Botticelli, Watteau, Delacroix and Ingrès. The château opened as a museum in 1898, a year after the duke's death. The Grands Appartements are in the Renaissance wing of the Petit Château, adjacent to the main building, and include the charming Grande Singerie, an 18th-century boudoir decorated with images of monkeys and chinoiserie. The fine gardens are the work of several masters, including the oldest areas which were designed by Frenchman André Le Notre.

Distance: 48km (30 miles)
Journey Time: 24 mins (SNCF train)/ 45 mins (RER train)
✉ Chantilly 60500 ☎ 03 44 27 31 80
🕐 Château: Apr–Oct daily 10–6; Nov–Mar 10.30–5. Closed early–late Jan. Grand Stables and Musée du Cheval: same as Château
🚆 Chantilly-Gouvieux SNCF, RER line D; free bus from station to château 💰 Expensive

The delightful Château de Chantilly

A winged statue in the Temple of Love, in the grounds of the Château de Chantilly

DISNEYLAND® PARIS

disneylandparis.com

Disneyland® Paris attracts millions of visitors from countries all around Europe and beyond to its two Parks—Disneyland® Park and Walt Disney Studios® Park. The resort, in the Marne-la-Vallée countryside east of Paris, opened in 1992. The Walt Disney Studios® Park was added in 2002. Other attractions include the Disney Village entertainment complex, seven hotels and even a golf course. Even so, Disney has announced a major expansion due to take place in the early 2020s.

Disneyland® Paris offers the traditional Disney experience with family-friendly attractions such as Main Street USA, with its re-creation of small-town America in the early 20th century, featuring a steam train and horse-drawn streetcars. There are rides to suit all ages and levels of bravery, from the charming musical journey of "it's a small world" to the lavish Indiana Jones™ and the Temple of Peril ride and Buzz Lightyear Laser

Blast—a laser shoot-out. Other white-knuckle rides include Star Wars Hyperspace Mountain and Big Thunder Mountain, a journey on a runaway mine train. Minimum height and age restrictions apply on some rides. Every evening (weather permitting), there's a spectacular live show with Disney characters old and new, and the sky is lit up with fireworks and laser lights, all set against the backdrop of the iconic and dreamlike Sleeping Beauty Castle.

Walt Disney Studios® Park's scarier rides include the terrifying Twilight Zone Tower of Terror™, an abandoned art deco hotel in which the elevator plummets faster than the speed of gravity.

Much of what there is to see in Walt Disney Studios® Park is movie-related and includes Paris's very own Gallic Disney attraction Ratatouille: A Recipe for Adventure, a 4-D experience where you can join talented gastronome Remy the Rat and his sidekick Linguini as they try to outwit Chef Skinner in Gasteau's restaurant. A host of Marvel Avengers attractions open in 2020, including an Iron Man-themed roller-coaster and a Spider-Man attraction. The movie theme continues with the extraordinary Moteurs...Action! Stunt Show Spectacular. Toon Studio is all about animation. At Art of Disney Animation®, you'll learn the techniques used to animate a Disney cartoon before getting the opportunity to try it for yourself.

Distance: 44km (27 miles)
Journey Time: 35 mins
✉ Marne-la-Vallée, 77777, Cedex 4
☎ 0825 300 500   🚉 RER Line A, Marne-la-Vallée   💶 Expensive

Sleeping Beauty's Castle

FONTAINEBLEAU

chateaudefontainebleau.fr

Fontainebleau has witnessed momentous events, including the birth of Louis XIII in 1601 and Napoleon signing his deed of abdication in 1814. Kings went hunting in the forest here as far back as the 12th century.

With more than 1,500 rooms and 53ha (130 acres) of parkland, the royal château of Fontainebleau is, despite its associations with *la chasse*, no mere hunting lodge: It was the only royal and imperial residence in France to be inhabited continuously for seven centuries, and is consequently a showcase for French architecture in the grand style. The surviving medieval keep forms the core of the building, which was extended in splendid Renaissance style under François I and later, in the 17th century, during the reign of Henri IV. A further wing was built during the time of Louis XV; after the Revolution, the château was restored by Napoleon Bonaparte. Its final royal inhabitant was Napoleon III, whose court stayed here until 1869.

The most spectacular of the interiors are the Renaissance rooms, inspired by the new artistic styles François I had seen while he was in Italy. These rooms include the sumptuous ballroom and François I's magnificent long gallery. Altogether more intimate in scale are Marie Antoinette's boudoirs and the apartment of Louis XIV's secret second wife, Madame de Maintenon. Outside, the beautiful Grand Parterre is reputedly the largest formal garden in Europe.

Distance: 68km (42 miles)
Journey Time: 50 mins
☎ 01 60 71 50 70 🕐 Château: Apr–Sep Wed–Mon 9.30–6; Oct–Mar Wed–Mon 9.30–5. Last admission 45 mins before closing. Courtyard and gardens: May–Sep daily 9–7; Mar–Apr, Oct 9–6; Nov–Feb 9–5. Park: daily 24 hours 🚉 Fontainebleau–Avon 🚌 PARISCityVISION runs day tours by coach, departing from rue des Pyramides, 75001 (tel 01 44 55 60 00, pariscityvision.com) 🎟 Château (limited areas only) moderate; courtyard, gardens and park free

Renaissance-style splendor at Fontainebleau

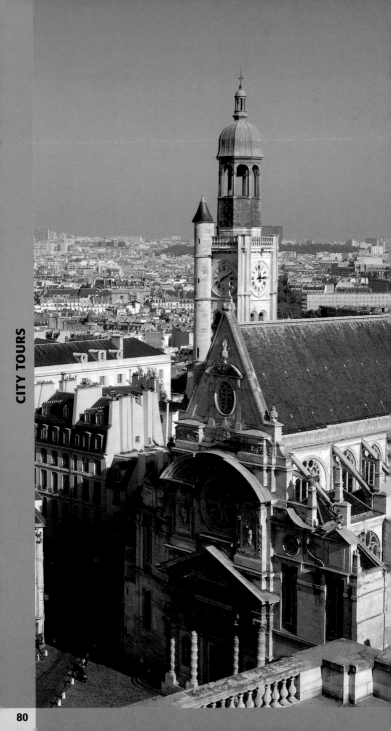

City Tours

This section contains self-guided tours that will help you explore the sights in each of the city's regions. Each tour is designed to take a day, with a map pinpointing the recommended places along the way. There is a quick reference guide at the end of each tour, listing everything you need in that region, so you know exactly what's close by.

Around the Tour Eiffel

Long vistas and grandiose public buildings characterize this part of Paris—but at its heart the Eiffel Tower is 324m (1,063ft) of pure, unmissable fun.

Morning

Start in front of the **Musée d'Orsay** (above, ▷ 38–39), but save the museum itself for another day. The Musée national de la Légion d'Honneur across the street sets the tone for a walk that's rich in political and military landmarks. Continue along the quai Anatole France to the Assemblée Nationale, France's lower house of parliament, its dignified neoclassical portico facing the **place de la Concorde** (▷ 50–51) across the river. Continue along quai d'Orsay past the mansion-like ministry of foreign affairs, popularly known by its address and one of the most important architectural monuments of the Second Empire. Until 1973 it was also a residence for high officials; King Juan Carlos of Spain was the last to stay there. Admire the florid, gilded statuary of the **Pont Alexandre III** (▷ 74) before turning left down broad, stately avenue du Maréchal Galliéni, named for a World War I military commander. Ahead of you is the wide, imposing facade of **Les Invalides** (▷ 22–23) which was built by Louis XIV and is the last resting place of Napoleon Bonaparte.

Late morning

Take time to explore the **Musée de l'Armée** (▷ 22), which occupies much of the majestic Les Invalides, before visiting France's national military pantheon, the **Église du Dôme** (right, ▷ 22–23), in which Napoleon's tomb takes pride of place.

Lunch

There's a simple but strategically located café on the south side of the Musée de l'Armée, but for a more substantial lunch in elegant surroundings make a short detour to the **Brasserie Thoumieux** (▷ 146) in rue Saint-Dominique.

Afternoon

Stroll the short distance along avenue de Tourville to reach the enormous École Militaire, constructed during the time of Louis XV and, today, still occupied by the military. It faces the **Parc du Champ de Mars** (left, ▷ 73), a vast green space stretching northwest toward the Eiffel Tower. To reach the park, cross the broad cobbled avenue de la Motte-Picquet with care. Amble the length of the Champs de Mars to reach the **Eiffel Tower** (below, ▷ 60–61); buy your tickets in advance online to save time.

Late afternoon

No visit to the Eiffel Tower is complete without crossing the river to experience the classic view of the tower itself. Cross the Pont d'Iéna to reach the **Palais de Chaillot** (▷ 72); save its museums for another day, but go up to the piazza between the two curved wings of the complex for the best view.

Evening

Stick around until after dusk to experience the beauty of the tower's soft golden lighting—and the spectacle of 20,000 flashing lights that make it glitter for five minutes every hour on the hour.

Around the Tour Eiffel
Quick Reference Guide

Les Invalides (▷ 22)
Commissioned by Louis XIV as a military hospital and welfare center, this magnificent complex houses the Army Museum and the tomb of Napoleon Bonaparte.

Musée d'Orsay (▷ 38)
The architectural merit of this audacious conversion of a former railroad station still divides opinion, but its breathtaking French art and sculpture collection makes it one of Paris's must-see attractions.

Musée du quai Branly – Jacques Chirac (▷ 40)
The national collection of art from Africa, Asia, Oceania and the Americas is housed in a modernist building by architect Jean Nouvel.

Musée Rodin (▷ 42)
An 18th-century mansion and its peaceful garden are the setting for the sculptures left to the nation by Rodin, along with other works by him and his contemporaries.

Tour Eiffel (▷ 60)
Though it was originally built as a temporary structure for the 1889 Exposition Universelle, it's hard to imagine Paris now without Gustave Eiffel's instantly recognizable tower.

CITY TOURS

MORE TO SEE   64

Catacombes de Paris
Musée d'Art Moderne de la Ville
   de Paris
Musée Yves Saint Laurent
Palais de Chaillot
Parc du Champ de Mars

Pont Alexandre III
Pont de l'Alma
Tour Montparnasse

SHOP   118

Antiques
Galerie Captier
Department Stores
Le Bon Marché Rive Gauche

Home and Garden
Au Bain Marie
Jewelry
Naïla de Monbrison

ENTERTAINMENT   130

Clubs
The Club

EAT   140

Asian
Benkay
French-Bistro
L'Affriolé
Bistrotters
French-Brasserie
Brasserie Thoumieux

French-Elegant
Le Jules Verne
French-Regional
L'Ami Jean

Palais de Tokyo courtyard at Musée d'Art Moderne de la Ville de Paris

Latin Quarter, St-Germain and Islands

The area's literary and philosophical associations lend intellectual luster to this tour of the Left Bank; fashion and fine dining bring Parisian élan to the mix; and the loveliness of the Seine and its islands adds a final dash of romance.

CITY TOURS

Morning

Start at rue Mouffetard, where the food and wine shops ensure a bustling atmosphere from morning onward. Make your way to the church of **Saint Étienne-du-Mont** (right, ▷ 67), worth a quick peek for its flamboyant late Gothic choir, before visiting the **Panthéon** (▷ 73), whose neo-classical dome dominates the Latin Quarter—Paris's university district. A stroll down rue Soufflot brings you to the main entrance of the **Jardin du Luxembourg** (▷ 24–25). At this leafy city park, do as the locals do and read in the sun.

Mid-morning

Leave the park by the exit on busy rue de Vaugirard, then follow the gently curving rue Servandoni and rue Palatine to reach **Église Saint-Sulpice** (left, ▷ 68), another Left Bank church well worth a look—this time for its vast, cathedral-like internal dimensions. From here to the boulevard St-Germain the streets are full of intriguing boutiques; indulge in a spot of window-shopping at the stores of talented French designers, then polish your intellectual credentials with a leisurely drink on the terrace of **Café Les Deux Magots** (▷ 66) or **Café de Flore** (▷ 66)—these famous cafés were once the haunts of the likes of Jean-Paul Sartre and Simone de Beauvoir.

Late morning

The church of **Saint-Germain-des-Prés** (right, ▷ 67) gives its name to one of Paris's most atmospheric quarters, wedged between boulevard St-Germain and the river. The streets are lined with handsome houses and dotted with art galleries and antiques shops; tucked into rue de Furstenberg is the Musée national Eugène Delacroix.

Lunch

This is an excellent part of town in which to break for lunch. There's plenty to tempt you, including the big brasserie buzz of **Alcazar** (▷ 144) or the fusion cuisine of **Ze Kitchen Galerie** (▷ 151)—both innovative and convivial lunchtime retreats.

Afternoon

Follow rue Dauphine to the **Pont Neuf** (▷ 74), crossing to the Île de la Cité to soak up the sun in the beautiful **square du Vert-Galant** (▷ 75), a tiny park on the island's western tip that offers wonderful views along the Seine. Afterwards, skirt the Île's north bank past the brooding bulk of the **Conciergerie** (▷ 18–19), a former royal palace, fortress and prison. Like the church of **Sainte-Chapelle** (▷ 56–57), it now forms part of the Palais de Justice. Slow the pace to admire the colors of the **Marché aux Fleurs** (▷ 127) before turning down rue de la Cité to reach the cathedral of **Notre-Dame** (▷ 44–45).

Late afternoon

The cathedral is currently closed to visitors due to the fire damage. Instead, admire the flying buttresses from outside and find the small copper Point Zero des Routes de France, from where all French map distances are measured.

Evening

The soft light of evening casts a particularly alluring spell over the **Île Saint-Louis** (▷ 68), for many visitors one of Paris's most romantic corners. Stroll its embankments to enjoy views of Notre-Dame and the Seine before crossing back to the Left Bank for dinner at **La Tour d'Argent** (right, ▷ 151).

TOUR D'ARGENT

Arc de Triomphe du Carrousel
Pyramide du Louvre
Rue St-Honoré

5

Musée du Louvre

QUAI FRANÇOIS MITTERRAND

St-Germain l'Auxerrois

Pont Royal

QUAI VOLTAIRE

Seine

QUAI DU LOUVRE

Pont des Arts

Seine Boat Trip

Pont Neuf (La Monnaie)

Pont Neuf

QUAI MALAQUAIS

QUAI DE CONTI

Institut de France

Square du Vert-Galant

Quai de l'Horloge

Palais de Justice

Rue de Beaune
Rue de Lille
Rue de Verneuil
Rue de l'Université

QUAI DES ORFÈVRES

6

Rue Jacob

Rue des Beaux-Arts
Rue de Seine
Rue Mazarine
Rue Guénégaud

Monnaie de Paris

QUAI DES GRANDS AUGUSTINS

Sainte-Chapelle

ST-GERMAIN-DES-PRÉS

R du Pré aux Clercs
Rue Jacob
Rue Visconti

Musée national Eugène Delacroix
R de l'Abbaye

Alcazar

Ze Kitchen Galerie
Rue Dauphine
Rue Christine
Rue de Savoie

Rue St-André-des-Arts

Sainte-Michel

BLVD Café de Flore & Café Les Deux Magots

Maison de Verre

Sonia Rykiel

ST-GERMAIN

Saint-Germain-des-Prés

Saint-Germain-des-Prés

R Gozlin

Rue de Buci
Rue de l'Ancienne Comédie

Rue Suger

St-Michel
St-Coeur

Rue de Sèvres
Rue du Dragon

BOULEVARD

Rue de Seine

Rue Danton

ST-MICHEL

Rue de Rennes
Rue Bonaparte
Rue du Four

Mabillon
R Clément
Rue Lobineau

ST-GERMAIN

Odéon

Rue de Condé
Rue de l'École de Médecine

Musée de Cluny Musée national du Moyen-Âge

7

Rue du Cherche-Midi

Rue du Vieux Colombier

Saint-Sulpice

Saint-Sulpice
Rue St-Sulpice
Place St-Sulpice
Rue Palatine

Rue Mabillon
Rue Garancière

Rue de Condé
R de l'Odéon
R Casimir Delavigne
Rue Monsieur-le-Prince

Rue Racine

BOULEVARD

Rue Champollion
Rue des Écoles

La Sorbonne

Rue Coëtlogon
Rue de Mézières
Rue Cassette
Rue Madame
Rue Férou
Rue Servandoni
Rue de Tournon

Place de l'Odéon

Rue de la Sorbonne

Rue de Vaugirard

Rue de Vaugirard

Place de la Sorbonne
Rue Cujas

Palais du Luxembourg

Rue de Médicis

Rue Soufflot

ST-JACQUES

8

Rue de Fleurus

Rue Guynemer

Jardin du Luxembourg

Luxembourg (Sénat) (RER)

Rue Royer-Collard
Rue Gay-Lussac

BLVD RASPAIL

Notre-Dame-des-Champs

Rue d'Assas
Rue Vavin
Rue Bréa

Rue Auguste Comte

ST-MICHEL

Rue de l'Abbé de l'Épée

Rue des Fossés St-Jacques

Rue Pierre et Marie Curie

0 _____ 500 m
0 _____ 500 yds

Rue Michelet
Avenue de l'Observatoire

BOULEVARD

Rue Gay-Lussac
Rue Louis Thuillier
Rue des Ursulines
Rue des Feuillantines

9

Vavin

Rue Notre-Dame-des-Champs
Rue Joseph Bara
Rue Le Verrier
Rue Henri Barbusse
Rue du Val de Grâce

BLVD RASPAIL

BOULEVARD DU MONTPARNASSE

G

Port-Royal (RER)

H

Latin Quarter, St-Germain and Islands
Quick Reference Guide

SIGHTS AND EXPERIENCES

CITY TOURS

Conciergerie (▷ 18)
Part medieval palace, part prison, this austere place preserves poignant memories of the victims of the French Revolution, including Marie-Antoinette.

Jardin du Luxembourg (▷ 24)
The epitome of French landscaping, this garden was commissioned by Marie de Médicis in 1615 and designed to remind her of her childhood Florentine home.

Musée de Cluny – Musée national du Moyen-Âge (▷ 30)
A turreted 15th-century mansion provides an appropriate setting for the national collection of medieval and Gothic art.

Notre-Dame (▷ 44)
Regardless of fire damage, admire the French Gothic architecture of this famous cathedral, part of UNESCO's "Paris, Banks of the Seine" World Heritage site.

Sainte-Chapelle (▷ 56)
Hidden within the Palais de Justice is a delicate late Gothic gem: Louis IX's soaring royal chapel, with a star-studded roof and breathtaking stained glass.

Seine Boat Trip (▷ 58)
Your feet will appreciate the rest as you watch the most important sights of Paris float gently by on a romantic one-hour boat trip along the River Seine.

Marais and Bastille

Contemporary art meets high fashion in Paris's trendiest district, yet alongside the *branché* (hippest) boutiques and bars the Marais preserves magnificent architecture and is the heart of the city's Jewish life.

Morning

Start with a late breakfast on the terrace at the chic **Café Beaubourg** (▷ 66) and ponder the audacious design of the **Centre Georges Pompidou** (above, ▷ 16–17), which caused quite a stir with its exposed ductwork and glass-roofed escalators when it opened in 1977. Today isn't the day to visit; instead, admire the jaunty Fontaine Stravinsky before walking the length of the museum, turning right into rue Rambuteau to reach the **Musée d'Art et d'Histoire du Judaïsme** (▷ 69) on rue du Temple. Housed in a grand 17th-century mansion or *hôtel particulier*, the museum documents European Jewish history and art from the Middle Ages onward.

Late morning

Rue Rambuteau runs into rue des Francs-Bourgeois, graced by more aristocratic town houses. Turn left up **rue Vieille-du-Temple** (▷ 75) to discover some of the Marais' hip designer stores, including **Vanessa Bruno** (▷ 129) at No.100, now a temple to shopping. Turn right into rue Debelleyme and right again to reach the **Musée national Picasso-Paris** (▷ 36–37), housed in another mansion, the elegant Hôtel Salé. Continue along rue Thorigny to rue Elzévir, where the 16th-century Hôtel Donon houses the **Musée Cognacq-Jay** (▷ 70), whose 18th-century paintings and *objets d'art* were assembled by the owner of the Samaritaine department store. Back on rue des Francs-Bourgeois, the Hôtel Carnavalet also dates from the 16th century and comprises one half of Paris's splendid museum of local history, the **Musée Carnavalet** (▷ 70). Admire the exterior architecture (the interior is currently closed for renovations).

Lunch

If the Marais' trendy shops have drained your funds, the inexpensive Jewish restaurants along **rue des Rosiers** (▷ 75) will be a welcome sight. **L'As du Fallafel** (▷ 145) at No. 34 is generally reckoned to serve the best falafel (mashed chickpeas formed into a ball and deep fried) in the city, but don't come here on Saturday—it's closed.

Afternoon

Retrace your steps to rue des Francs-Bourgeois, continuing as far as **place des Vosges** (▷ 52–53). This beautiful formal square dates from the early 17th century and is the best preserved in Paris; in the southeast corner, Victor Hugo's house is now a museum. Rue de Birague leads from the south side of the square to busy rue Saint-Antoine; to the left is the place de la Bastille, former site of the infamous prison and now dominated by the ultramodern **Opéra Bastille** (▷ 138). To the right, the Hôtel de Béthune-Sully is among the most magnificent of all the Marais' mansions; you can't visit the interior—now occupied by the Ministry of Culture—but you can admire the court and elegant garden. Continue along rue Saint-Antoine and rue François-Miron to reach the **Mémorial de la Shoah** (below, ▷ 69), on rue Geoffroy l'Asnier—a somber counterpoint to the Musée d'Art et d'Histoire du Judaïsme.

Dinner

Bofinger (▷ 146) is one of Paris's most historic brasseries and a memorable spot for dinner. Afterward, stay in the Marais for a drink in one of the area's lively cafés and bars—many of them popular with the city's LGBTQ+ community.

SIGHTS AND EXPERIENCES

Centre Georges Pompidou (▷ 16)

The museum houses the large national collection of modern and contemporary art, from fauvism, cubism and surrealism to Pop Art and works by the stars of this art scene. The building includes a library, cinema, bookshops and a chic restaurant.

Musée national Picasso-Paris (▷ 36)

Some 500 works by Picasso are displayed in this historic Marais mansion, following a thorough refurbishment that has tripled the exhibition area and improved access for visitors with disabilities. It boasts one of the world's finest collections of work by the artist.

Place des Vosges (▷ 52)

Dating from 1612 and built on the site of a 14th-century royal palace that was abandoned and demolished by Catherine de' Medici after her husband Henri II died there, this handsome square of arcaded houses overlooks a central garden. Famous former residents include Victor Hugo.

CITY TOURS

CITY TOURS

Louvre and Champs-Élysées

Dress to impress for this route through the very heart of Paris, where iconic landmarks and glamorous designer shopping ensure there's plenty of interest along the way.

Morning
Start with a late breakfast on the terrace of the **Café Marly** (▷ 146) at the **Louvre** (▷ 32–33). You'll probably want to set aside another day to see the collection but this is a fine vantage point from which to admire the splendid setting and the audacity of I.M. Pei's modernist glass pyramid. Cross the busy place du Carrousel du Louvre to reach the Arc de Triomphe du Carrousel—not the famous triumphal arch but a smaller version, Roman in its inspiration and built in 1805 to celebrate Napoleon's victories. Beyond it, there's a dramatic view along Paris's monumental axis—west through the **Jardin des Tuileries** (below, ▷ 26–27), across the **place de la Concorde** (▷ 50–51) and up the avenue des Champs-Élysées to the Arc de Triomphe and the distant **Grande Arche** (▷ 76) at La Défense. Paris's most central park, the Jardin des Tuileries has been a UNESCO World Heritage Site since 1991. Two galleries—the **Orangerie** (▷ 71–72) and **Jeu de Paume** (▷ 51)—offer an excellent excuse to linger a while.

Mid-morning
Leave the Jardin des Tuileries at the Carrousel du Louvre exit and cross rue de Rivoli, walking straight ahead along the avenue de l'Opera. Turn right into rue Richelieu and immediately on your right is the ornate facade of the **Comédie-Française** (▷ 136), famed for its classical theater. Behind the building, discover the historic gardens of the **Domaine national du Palais-Royal** (▷ 67). Return to avenue de l'Opera and turn right into rue Saint-Honoré to browse and window-shop. No. 233 is home to luggage-maker **Goyard** (▷ 126). At the corner of place Vendôme (top right), look for one of the most elegant squares in the city, with a 44m (144ft) bronze column in its center.

Beyond rue Royale, rue Saint-Honoré becomes rue du Faubourg Saint-Honoré, home to the Élysée palace—the official residence of the French president—and also to some of Paris's most chic designer boutiques. Avenue Matignon then continues the luxury theme but features fine art galleries and antiques dealers instead of upscale fashion stores.

Lunch
Take a table on the terrace at **L'Avenue** (▷ 145) on avenue Montaigne for good bistro food and some first-class people-watching; this is Parisian chic at its best.

Afternoon
The window-shopping shifts up a gear on the far side of the Rond Point des Champs-Élysées along avenue Montaigne. Here, **Dior** (▷ 125) and **Chanel** (▷ 124) both have splendid flagship stores in which to lose half a day, and the array of designer labels is enough to constitute a serious hazard to your bank balance. Turn right off avenue Montaigne up rue François 1er to reach the broad avenue des Champs-Élysées, Paris's most famous boulevard (left). It ends at place de l'Étoile, dominated by the stately bulk of the **Arc de Triomphe** (▷ 14–15). Quite aside from its significance as a national monument, the Arc also makes an excellent platform for views across the city.

1

Parc de Monceau

Rue de la Comtesse de Ségur

Musée Cernuschi

Monceau

Courcelles

Place des Ternes

AVENUE DES TERNES

BOULEVARD DE COURCELLES

Musée Nissim de Camondo

Ternes

AVENUE HOCHE

Rue de Lisbonne

Rue de Lisbonne

Rue de la Bienfaisance

2

AVENUE DE FRIEDLAND

BOULEVARD HAUSSMANN

Musée Jacquemart-André

Miromesnil

PLACE CHARLES DE GAULLE

Charles de Gaulle Étoile (+RER)

Arc de Triomphe

CHAMPS-ÉLYSÉES

ST-HONORÉ

Saint Philippe du Roule

3

George V

AVENUE DES CHAMPS-ÉLYSÉES

Palais de l'Élysée

Rond-Point des Champs-Élysées Marcel Dassault

Franklin D Roosevelt

4

Musée Baccarat

l'Avenue   Chanel

Impasse d'Antin

Champs-Élysées-Clemenceau

Jardin des Champs-Élysée

Musée Galliéra

Musée Yves Saint Laurent

Dior

Palais de la Découverte

Grand Palais

Petit Palais

AVENUE DU PRÉSIDENT WILSON

6 New York

Cours Albert 1er

Cours Albert 1er

VOIE

GEORGES

POMPIDOU

Cours La Reine

Cours La Reine

Palais de Tokyo

Musée d'Art Moderne de la Ville de Paris

Pont de l'Alma

Les Berges

Pont Alexandre III

Seine

AVENUE DE NEW YORK

Pont de l'Alma (RER)

QUAI D'ORSAY

Invalides (+RER)

Assemblée nationale

5

QUAI BRANLY

Musée du quai Branly - Jacques Chirac

Rue de l'Université

AVENUE RAPP

AVENUE DE LA BOURDONNAIS

AVENUE BOSQUET

Esplanade des Invalides

Rue St-Dominique

6

Tour Eiffel

La Tour Maubourg

RUE DE GRENELLE

Les Invalides

Varenne

Musée Rodin

7

Parc du Champ de Mars

PLACE JOFFRE

École Militaire

AVENUE DE TOURVILLE

BOULEVARD DES INVALIDES

INVALIDES

Saint François-Xavier

Jardin Nicole de Hauteclocque

B   **C**   **D**   **E**

Rome

DES BATIGNOLLES

PIGALLE

Place de l'Europe

GARE
SAINT-LAZARE

**Musée
Gustave
Moreau**

BOULEVARD HAUSSMANN

BOULEVARD HAUSSMANN

**Palais
Garnier**

**Passages
Couverts**

Musée
Grévin

**Musée du
Parfum
Fragonard**

OPÉRA

BLVD MONTMARTRE

BOULEVARD DES ITALIENS

Église de la
Madeleine

BLVD DE LA MADELEINE

BOULEVARD DES CAPUCINES

**Théâtre Musée
des Capucines**

RUE DU QUATRE SEPTEMBRE

**La
Bourse**

**Bibliothèque
nationale
de France**

**Galerie
Colbert**

**Galerie
Vivienne**

Goyard

**Domaine
national
du Palais-Royal**

**Place de la
Concorde**

Jeu de
Paume

Bassin
Octogonal

RUE DE RIVOLI

Esplanade des Feuillants

**Musée de
l'Orangerie**

*Jardin des
Tuileries*

**Musée des
Arts Décoratifs**

**Comédie
Française**

Palais-
Royal

Galerie
Véro-Dodat

Jardin du
Carrousel

Palais-Royal
Musée du
Louvre

RUE DE RIVOLI

Galerie
Véro-Dodat

Palais
Bourbon

Assemblée
nationale

Musée d'Orsay

**Musée
d'Orsay**

**Arc de Triomphe
du Carrousel**

**Pyramide
du Louvre**

Musée du Louvre

St-Germain
l'Auxerrois

QUAI FRANÇOIS MITTERRAND

Seine

**Pont
des Arts**

**Seine
Boat Trip**

**Pont
Neuf**

QUAI VOLTAIRE

QUAI MALAQUAIS

QUAI DE CONTI

**Rue
Jacob**

Institut
de France

**Square du
Vert-Galant**

Musée de
la Monnaie

Palais
de Justice

0 ——— 500 m

0 ——— 500 yds

BLVD ST-GERMAIN

**ST-GERMAIN-
DES-PRÉS**

**Café de Flore
& Café Les Deux Magots**

Maison
de Verre

**Musée national
Eugène Delacroix**

**Saint-Germain-
des-Prés**

BOULEVARD ST-GERMAIN

**Musée de Cluny –
Musée national du
Moyen-Âge**

Rue du
Cherche-Midi

**Saint-
Sulpice**

F

G

H

SIGHTS AND EXPERIENCES

Arc de Triomphe (▷ 14)

With 12 of Haussmann's avenues radiating from it, this arch is the focus of national pride and a memorial to France's war dead, with a Memorial Flame at its base.

Galerie Vivienne and the Passages Couverts (▷ 20)

A network of 19th-century shopping arcades allows you to stroll and people-watch under cover.

Jardin des Tuileries (▷ 26)

First laid out in the 16th century, this is one of the most popular parks for Parisians. It is a delightful place in which to stop and relax.

Musée du Louvre (▷ 32)

The world's largest museum is a dazzling experience, from the modernist glass pyramid over its entrance to the world-famous treasures it contains.

Palais Garnier (▷ 46)

Charles Garnier's wedding cake of a building is as sumptuous as an opera house should be, with a foyer and grand staircase every bit as majestic as the auditorium itself.

Place de la Concorde (▷ 50)

A maelstrom of traffic today, this vast open space was the site of the gruesome guillotine and many public executions during the French Revolution.

CITY TOURS

Montmartre

There's art, raffish nightlife, picturesque views and stepped streets in this remarkably village-like corner of the city.

Morning

Wear comfortable shoes—the route is mostly downhill and avoids steps as far as possible, but this is still the highest point in the city; the slopes can be steep and the streets are cobbled in places. Take the Métro to Abbesses station; it's the city's deepest, with an original art nouveau canopy. Window-shop your way from **place des Abbesses** (▷ 73–74) past small boutiques in rue Yvonne le Tac and rue Tardieu to reach the funicular. One of the area's celebrated stepped streets runs parallel to it, but the railway is easier on your feet. Journey's end is the distinctive, white hilltop basilica of **Sacré-Cœur** (right, ▷ 54–55). It's one of Paris's most visited attractions and the crush inside can sometimes mar the experience. What doesn't disappoint is the breath-taking view over the city—whether from the dome or from the terrace in front of the church.

Late morning

Follow rue du Cardinal Guibert along the side of the church, braving the busy rue Chevalier de la Barre to reach calmer, prettier rue Cortot. Here, the **Musée de Montmartre** (▷ 71) documents the history and artistic associations of the area, which in the 19th century became a popular place of entertainment. Continue along rue Cortot to the junction with rue des Saules—if you haven't already caught a glimpse of Montmartre's vineyard, it's just downhill to the right. Turn uphill along rue des Saules then left into rue Norvins to reach busy place du Tertre, famous for its portrait painters (left).

Lunch

This is an unashamedly touristy part of Montmartre, with no shortage of places to eat, though there are many cafés with daily menus of variable quality; **Au Clair de la Lune** (▷ 145) in rue Poulbot is one of the nicest options, tucked away off place du Tertre. In summer, arrive early to make sure you get one of the tables outside.

Afternoon

From rue Poulbot, turn left down rue Norvins to reach the Radet, the first of Montmartre's windmills, at the top of rue Lepic; there were once 14 but now this and the nearby Blute Fin are the last survivors. Together they constitute the Moulin de la Galette (right), which during its time as a dance hall was painted by Renoir. It is now a restaurant. Continue downhill on rue Lepic, turning sharply right at its junction with rue des Abbesses to reach the **Cimetière de Montmartre** (▷ 66–67), where the roll call of famous names rivals that of Père Lachaise.

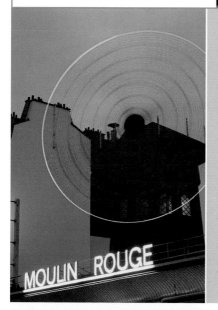

Evening

Rue des Abbesses and the surrounding streets hum with life in the evening; catch a film at **Studio 28** (▷ 139), enjoy dinner at **Seb'on** (▷ 151) or dinner and a show at **Michou** (▷ 138). Later and much livelier nightlife—from rock concerts to discos and sleazy sex clubs—is found at the foot of rue des Martyrs on place Pigalle and boulevard de Clichy, the latter dominated by the famous **Moulin Rouge** (left, ▷ 138) club.

Square Carpeaux

Rue Legendre
Rue d'Oslo
Rue Coysevox
Rue Carpeaux
Rue
Marcadet

Rue Davy
Rue Lamarck
Rue Carpeaux
Rue Lamarck

AVENUE DE ST-OUEN
Rue Etex
Rue Lamarck
Rue Lamarck

Rue Legendre
Rue du Capitaine Madon
Villa St-Michel
Rue de la Barrière Blanche
Rue Joseph de Maistre
Eugène Carrière
Félix Ziem
Rue Damrémont

Rue Dautancourt
Rue Fauvet
Rue Gannèron

① AVENUE DE CLICHY
R Etienne Jodelle

Avenue Junot
Rue Simon Dereure

La Fourche
R Pierre Ginier
Rue Hégésippe Moreau
Rue Gannèron

Avenue Junot
Rue Lepic
Le Moulin de la Galette

Cimetière de Montmartre
Rue Tourlaque
Rue Caulaincourt

Square de la Rue Burq

Rue Hélène
Rue Lemercier
AVENUE DE CLICHY
Rue Cavallotti
Rue Gannèron

R Joseph de Maistre
Rue Lepic
Rue Constance
Studio 28
Rue Durantin

Rue des Dames
Rue Lécluse
Rue Capron
Rue Forest
P P
Rue Caulaincourt
Rue des Abbesses

Rue Biot
Rue Cauchois
Rue Robert Planquette
Rue Véron

② BOULEVARD DE CLICHY
Place de Clichy
R Pierre Haret
Rue de Douai
R de Bruxelles
Moulin Rouge
Rue Puget
Rue Coustou
Blanche
BOULEVARD DE
Pigalle

BOULEVARD DES BATIGNOLLES
RUE DE ST-PÉTERSBOURG
R de Florence
Rue de Bruxelles
Rue de Vintimille
Rue de Calais
Rue d'Amsterdam
Rue de Clichy
RUE BLANCHE
P
Rue Pierre Fontaine
Rue Duperré
Rue de Douai
Rue Fromentin

Rue de Turin
Rue Clapeyron
R de Parme
Rue Ballu

Place de Dublin
Rue Jules Lefebvre
Square Moncey
Rue Chaptal
Rue Paul Escudier
Rue Henner

③ Rue de Moscou
Rue de Turin
Liège
Rue de Liège
Rue de Liège
Rue Moncey
Rue La Bruyère
Pigalle
Rue La Bruyère
Rue Notre-Dame
Rue Henry Monnier

0   200 m
0   200 yds

Rue de Milan
Jean-Baptiste
Place St-Georges

RUE DE LONDRES
Rue d'Athènes
Rue de Clichy
RUE BLANCHE
Rue de la Tour des Dames
Rue d'Aumale
Musée Gustave Moreau

GARE SAINT-LAZARE
P
RUE DE LONDRES
Rue St-Lazare
St-Georges
Rue Taitbout

④ Saint-Lazare
ⓐ
RUE ST-LAZARE
Place d'Estienne d'Orves
Trinité (d'Estienne d'Orves)
RUE DE LA CHAUSSÉE D'ANTIN
ⓑ
RUE DE
Rue de la Victoire

Rue d'Amsterdam
Haussmann-Saint-Lazare (RER)

Square
Léon-Serpollet

Rue Marcadet

Marcadet-
Poissonniers

Rue   Ferdinand   Flocon

Rue   Ordener

Cenis

Hermel

Ramey

Rue Marcadet

Rue   du   Mont

Rue   Marcadet

Rue   Eugène   Sue

Rue Clignancourt

Rue Marcadet

Smirnott

BOULEVARD BARBÈS

Rue Dühesme

Rue de la
Fontaine
de Butte

Rue des Saules

Rue Francoeur

Rue du Baigneur

Rue Darwin

Rue de Labat

Rue Labat

Lamarck

Rue Caulaincourt

Rue Lamarck

Rue Custine

Rue Lecuyer

P

Rue de Clignancourt

Doudeauville

Cimetière
St-Vincent

Place
Constantin
Pecqueur

Rue Lamarck

Rue Paul Féval

Rue St-Vincent

Rue
Becquerel

Rue Bachelet

Rue Labat

Rue

Rue Nicolet

Rue   Poulet

Rue des Poissonniers

Château-
Rouge

Rue de
l'Abreuvoir

Rue de Saules

Square
S.-
son-
ncet

Rue de la Bonne

Ramey

Cuise

Rue Poulet

Myrha

**Musée de
Montmartre**

Rue Cortot

MONTMARTRE

Rue Norvins

Rue du

Chevalier
de la Barre

Rue Paul Albert

P Feutrier

Rue Lamarck

BOULEVARD BARBÈS

Place Jean-
Baptiste
Clément

Rue Lepic

Au Clair
de la Lune

Place du
Tertre

R du
Cardinal
Guibert

★
**Sacré-
Cœur**

Rue Muller

Rue Feutrier

Rue Christiani

Rue Azaïs

R du Cardinal Dubois

Rue André del Sarte

Rue Gabrielle

Rue Berthe

Funiculaire
Montmartre

R André Barsacq

Square
Louise
Michel

Rue Charles Nodier

Rue Ronsard

Rue de Clignancourt

Rue de Sofia

Rue Ravignan

Rue des Trois Frères

**Place des
Abbesses**

Rue la Vieuville

Rue Chappe

Rue Pierre Picard

Rue des Islettes

Abbesses

Rue Yvonne Le Tac

Place St-Pierre

Rue d'Orsel

Rue Houdon

Rue d'Orsel

Seb'on

Rue Tardieu

Rue d'Orsel

Rue Séveste

Rue Bellevonne

Rue des Martyrs

Rue des Trois Frères

Michou

DE   📷   Anvers
(Sacré Cœur)

ROCHECHOUART

Barbès-
Rochechouart

CLICHY

P

Square
d'Anvers

Place d'Anvers

Rue de Dunkerque

R de Rochechouart

Rue de Delta

BOULEVARD DE MAGENTA

BOULEVARD

Rue Bochart de Saron

Rue Lallier

Rue du   Faubourg

PIGALLE

Victor Massé

Avenue Trudaine

Rue Pétrelle

Rue de Dunkerque

Rue des Martyrs

Rue Rodier

Rue Turgot

Rue de Rochechouart

Rue Lamartine

Rue Condorcet

Rue de Navarin

Rue Rodier

Rue de la Tour d'Auvergne

Rue Condorcet

Rue de Maubeuge

Rue d'Abbeville

Rue de Rocroy

Rue Clauzel

aternel

Rue des Martyrs

Rue Milton

R Manuel

R de Chantilly

Rue Pierre Sémard

Poissonnière

P

Saint-Georges

R de
Laferrière

Rue choron

Rue Bellefond

Rue du Faubourg

Poissonnière

Poissonnière

St-Lazare

Rue de Maubeuge

Rue Hippolyte Lebas

Rue Lamartine

R Mayran

P

Square de
Montholon

R Montholon

Rue des Messageries

Notre-Dame
de-Lorette

Rue Buffault

Cadet

RUE   LA   FAYETTE

R Montholon

R Papillon

CHÂTEAUDUN

Rue Bleue

Cité de
Trévise

Rue de Paradis

R de la Victoire

Le Peletier

Rue Cadet

Rue Saulnier

Rue de Trévise

(c)

(d)

Montmartre Quick Reference Guide

Sacré-Cœur (▷ 54)

Neo-Romanesque and Byzantine in style, the white basilica of Sacré-Cœur is one of the most familiar features of the Parisian skyline, looking down on the city from its lofty hilltop perch. Built as a memorial to the dead of the Franco-Prussian war and Paris Commune, it wasn't completed until the eve of World War I and was only consecrated in 1919. Its lovely stained-glass windows were destroyed during World War II and restored afterwards.

MORE TO SEE	64

Cimetière de Montmartre
Musée de Montmartre

Place des Abbesses

The interior of Sacré-Cœur

CITY TOURS

SHOP 118

Books and CDs
Librairie des Abbesses
Clothes and Hats
Petit Bateau

Concept Store
Le Sept Cinq
Markets
Marché Barbès
Marché de la rue Lepic

ENTERTAINMENT 130

Cinemas
Studio 28
Clubs
Michou

Contemporary Music
La Boule Noire/La Cigale Le Bus
Palladium
Divan du Monde
Shows
Moulin Rouge

EAT 140

French-Bistro
Au Virage Lepic
Le Progrès
Seb'on
French-Regional
Au Clair de la Lune

Italian/Mediterranean
Pink Mamma
Organic
Rose Bakery

CITY TOURS

Tomb of Alexandre Dumas in the Cimetière de Montmartre

Montmartre

Farther Afield

Louis XIV's palace at Versailles is one excursion not to miss, while more offbeat charm is to be found in the outer *arrondissements* of the city's north and east.

DAY 1
Morning
Take RER Line C to Versailles Rive Gauche and then stroll the short distance to the **Château de Versailles** (left, ▷ 62–63). Try for an early start—the château opens at 9—and buy your ticket online to avoid a long wait in line. Start with the Grands Appartements: Admire the bombastic painted ceiling of the exquisite Hall of Mirrors, which celebrates Louis XIV's military campaigns, before visiting the King's Apartment.

Lunch
If you're visiting on the weekend between April and October, exit into the gardens before midday to catch the Grandes Eaux fountains (right) performing to music; they do the same again from 3.30 to 5. Afterwards, stroll down to the Grand Canal where there are formal and informal lunch options—La Flottille (tel 01 39 51 41 58, laflottille.fr) has a garden terrace by the waterside.

Afternoon
Follow the route marked on the free map to reach the **Petit Trianon** (▷ 63). Closely associated with Marie-Antoinette, this country estate is for many the highlight of a visit to Versailles. Explore the twee Hameau de la Reine—a play village built for the queen's amusement—before continuing through formal gardens to reach the **Grand Trianon** (▷ 63), the colonnaded marble palace where Louis XIV enjoyed trysts with his mistress, Madame de Montespan.

DAY 2
Morning

Another early start, this time for a weekend stroll through the **Marché aux Puces de Saint-Ouen** (right, ▷ 28–29)—Paris's most famous flea market. Take Métro Line 4 to Porte de Clignancourt and cross under the Périphérique to get there by 10. Fortify yourself with coffee from one of the cafés along rue des Rosiers and pick up a free map from the tourist office at 7 impasse Simon by the Marché Paul Bert to navigate your way. Take a couple of hours to appreciate the sheer variety on offer, from secondhand clothes to elegant art deco furniture and fine art.

Lunch

Take the Métro to Barbès–Rochechouart, change to Line 2 (direction: Nation) and alight at Stalingrad. Admire the 18th-century Rotonde de la Villette and the views up the canal basin toward **Parc de la Villette** (▷ 76) before climbing hilly avenue Sécretan. Assemble a picnic from the covered market and shops here. Eat it in the **Parc des Buttes Chaumont** (left, ▷ 76) at the top of the hill—if you're lucky, you might get a hillock to yourself.

Afternoon

Descend avenue Mathurin Moreau to Colonel Fabien station. Take the Métro to Père Lachaise—there's a gate into the **Cimetière du Père Lachaise** (▷ 48–49) directly opposite, but the main entrance is farther along boulevard de Ménilmontant. Pick up a map to find the most-visited graves, including those of Oscar Wilde, Édith Piaf and Jim Morrison, but be sure to admire the extraordinary architecture of the many tombs, too.

Early evening

Stay in the area for an apéritif or relaxed early dinner in the very vibrant rue Oberkampf. For a contemporary French bistro experience, head to dinner at **Septime** (▷ 151) close by on rue de Charonne.

BOIS-COLOMBES

ASNIÈRES-SUR-SEINE

Seine

LA GARENNE-COLOMBES

CLICHY

La Grande Arche

COURBEVOIE

Île de la Jatte

LEVALLOIS-PERRET

LA DÉFENSE

NEUILLY-SUR-SEINE

AVENUE CHARLES DE GAULLE

BÂTIG

MONCEAU

Parc de Monceau

8e

BOULEVARD HAUSSMANN

Île de Puteaux

Fondation Louis Vuitton

ST-HONORÉ

AVENUE DES CHAMPS-ÉLYSÉES

Paris

ALLÉE DE LONGCHAMP

CHAMPS-ÉLYSÉES

Lac Inférieur

CHAILLOT

16e

Bois de Boulogne

Musée Marmottan Monet

Esplanade des Invalide

INVALIDES

Lac Supérieur

PASSY

Parc du Champ de Mars

7e

AUTOROUTE DE NORMANDIE

A13

E05

AUTEUIL

15e

GRENELLE

ROUTE DE LA REINE

Parc André-Citroën

VAUGIRARD

BOULOGNE-BILLANCOURT

Seine

BOULEVARD VICTOR

Parc Georges Brassens

★**Versailles**

Parc de l'Île St-Germain

Parc Suzanne Lenglen

BLVD LEFEBVRE

BOULEVARD BRUNE

BOULEVARD PÉRIPHÉRIQUE

Île St-Germain

ISSY-LES-MOULINEAUX

VANVES

Parc Frédéric Pic

MALAKOFF

MEUDON

MONTROUG

AVENUE DE PARIS

Cimetière Parisien de Bagneux

0   1 km
0   1 mile

ST-OUEN

D410

D14

D111

AUTOROUTE DU NORD

A1

Canal St-Denis

N301

N2

AUBERVILLIERS

AVENUE JEAN JAURÈS

Cimetière
Parisien de St-Ouen

**Marché aux Puces
de Saint-Ouen**

Cimetière
Parisien
de Pantin-
Bobigny

BOULEVARD PÉRIPHÉRIQUE

BOULEVARD PÉRIPHÉRIQUE

PANTIN

D115

BESSIÈRES

BOULEVARD

NEY

BLVD NEY

BOULEVARD
MACDONALD

AVENUE DE ST-OUEN

LICHY

Cimetière de
Montmartre

18e

LA
CHAPELLE

AVENUE DE FLANDRE

BLVD
SERURIER

**Parc de la
Villette**

LA
VILLETTE

19e

N3

LE PRÉ-
ST-GERVAIS

BLVD DE PÉRIPHÉRIQUE

NOLLES

MONTMARTRE

17e

AVENUE JEAN JAURÈS

PIGALLE

BOULEVARD DE MAGENTA

9e

10e

Canal St-Martin

Parc de la
Butte Rouge

**Parc des Buttes
Chaumont**

BOULEVARD MORTIER

E15

OPÉRA

2e

Jardin du
Palais
Royal

BOULEVARD DE SÉBASTOPOL

RÉPUBLIQUE

BELLEVILLE

Parc de
Belleville

20e

1er

Jardin
des Tuileries

LES
HALLES

RUE DE RIVOLI

3e

AVENUE DE LA RÉPUBLIQUE

Seine

LE
MARAIS

BLVD BEAUMARCHAIS

11e

ST-GERMAIN-
DES-PRÉS

Île de
la Cité

4e

Île
St-Louis

BASTILLE

CHARONNE

**Cimetière du
Père Lachaise**

6e

QUARTIER
LATIN

Jardin du
Luxembourg

5e

Jardin
des
Plantes

RUE DU FAUBOURG ST-ANTOINE

U MONTPARNASSE

BOULEVARD DE L'HÔPITAL

12e

BLVD SOULT

ONTPARNASSE

Cimetière du
Montparnasse

AVENUE DU MAINE

14e

LES GOBELINS

BOULEVARD
AUGUSTE BLANQUI

13e

Parc de
Bercy

QUAI DE BERCY

BERCY

Seine

BOULEVARD PONIATOWSKI

Bois de
Vincennes

ALÉSIA

Parc
Montsouris

BOULEVARD JOURDAN

BLVD KELLERMANN

Parc
Kellermann

BOULEVARD MASSÉNA

BOULEVARD PÉRIPHÉRIQUE

CHARENTON-
LE-PONT

A4 E50

AUTOROUTE DE L'EST

D920

E05

AUTOROUTE DU SOLEIL

A6a

A6b

AUTOROUTE DU SOLEIL

D7

GENTILLY

Cimetière
Parisien
d'Ivry

D5

IVRY-SUR-SEINE

E50

D19

D154

D19

SIGHTS AND EXPERIENCES

Marché aux Puces de Saint-Ouen (▷ 28)

The sprawling, 7ha (15-acre) Marché aux Puces de Saint-Ouen is not one market but a series of market buildings, arcades, stalls and individual dealers. Together they create an enjoyable way to spend a weekend morning mingling with the locals.

Musée Marmottan Monet (▷ 34)

This 19th-century mansion is an elegant setting for a truly mesmerizing collection of Impressionist paintings, including Monet's memorable and world-renowned canvases of dappled irises, wisteria and water lilies from his last years at Giverny.

Père Lachaise (▷ 48)

The chance to see the tombs of literary, musical and artistic greats—including Frederick Chopin, Marcel Proust and Oscar Wilde—is what draws many visitors to this historic cemetery in the east of the city. The wonderful architecture of its myriad tombs and vaults repays languid exploration.

Versailles (▷ 62)

The grandeur of the Sun King, Louis XIV, survives in swaggering stone form at the Château de Versailles, but the complex also offers more intimate glimpses of royal life at the estates of Grand and Petit Trianon. Despite the crowds, this rural idyll makes for a perfect day away from the city rush.

MORE TO SEE 64

Fondation Louis Vuitton
La Grande Arche
Parc André-Citroën
Parc des Buttes Chaumont
Parc de la Villette

ENTERTAINMENT 130

Classical Music
Philharmonie de Paris

EAT 140

French-Bistro
La Petite Ardoise
French-Elegant
Gordon Ramsay au Trianon
Septime

Modern design on a huge scale, La Grand Arche

Shop

Whether you're looking for the best local products, a department store or a quirky boutique, you'll find them all in Paris. In this section shops are listed alphabetically.

SHOP

Introduction

One of the world's shopping capitals, Paris is not all about luxury designer stores. Don't forget the individual shops, inexpensive chain stores, big and small flea markets and everything in between.

The Capital of Fashion

Narrow rue du Faubourg Saint-Honoré and broad, stately avenue Montaigne are the most prestigious fashion addresses in the city—the places to go for couture, luxury and high price tags, or simply for a spot of *lèche-vitrines* (window-shopping) past the beautiful displays. In these streets you'll find the top names—Gucci, Roberto Cavalli and Prada. Rue de la Paix glitters with names, including Cartier and Van Cleef et Arpels. To the north are the great Belle Époque department stores of boulevard Haussmann, Galeries Lafayette and Printemps, complete with English-speaking guides on hand.

Nip across the Seine to Saint-Germain-des-Prés for fashion with flair alongside fine art and antiques and, farther south, the city's oldest department store, Le Bon Marché Rive Gauche (▷ 124), at 24 rue de Sèvres.

The Capital of Chic

Be sure not to miss the historic *arrondissements* between the Louvre and Bastille. Fashion has colonized the area around place des Victoires in the 1st *arrondissement* with

---

GOURMET PICNICS

There isn't a word for delicatessen in French. A *charcuterie* mainly sells cold meats and a *traiteur* is a caterer or a shop selling ready-cooked dishes. The two are closely related and are often combined. Inside, glass cabinets or counters display dozens of exquisite freshly prepared salads, such as grated carrot, paper-thin slices of cucumber, aubergines (eggplant) and mushrooms, as well as meat pies and spicy sausages, garlic, bean-and-pork stew and a gourmet mix of cooked meats.

Clockwise from top: Tasty choices at Le Bon Marché Rive Gauche; the enticing façade of some of the city's chic shops; sweet treats from Stohrer chocolate

Christian Louboutin and Stella McCartney opening boutiques in the Palais Royal; farther east, rue Étienne-Marcel is good for youth-oriented labels, while rue Vieille-du-Temple in the Marais is a must-see for its mix of small boutiques and intriguing concept stores.

Out of the Rain
In the Sentier and Opéra districts, explore delightful, shop-lined 19th-century arcades, full of quirky and interesting small boutiques that make them an excellent place to linger if the weather is wet.

Buy the Best
Seek out great French flair and quality, not just in fashion but also in high-quality cookware—Le Creuset saucepans, Sabatier knives, kitchen gadgets that actually work, such as a Peugeot peppermill—and in stylish children's and baby clothes. For epicurean delights try exquisite prepared foods from Fauchon (▷ 125) or La Grande Épicerie at Le Bon Marché Rive Gauche, handmade chocolates and fine wines, which all make tempting buys.

Down to Earth
If luxury and high fashion are not for you there are bargains to be had, so join the locals at the legendary flea markets, starting with Marché aux Puces de Saint-Ouen (▷ 28–29).

WHAT'S WHAT
Boulangeries sell baguettes, and more besides; try the *ficelle*, a thinner, finer loaf, or *pain au levain*, delicious sourdough bread. And then there are the croissants, *ordinaire* or *au beurre* (with butter). *Pâtisseries* sell pastries and tarts. *Charcuteries* sell cold meats, snails, cheese, truffles, wines, caviar and more. *Parfumeries* can stock solely French perfume but some sell cosmetics and soaps, too. *Bouquinistes* sell used books, prints, posters and postcards.

and pastry shop; the latest shoe trends to tempt shoppers; a cheese made in France's Auvergne region, Bleu d'Auvergne, for sale in the city

SHOP

Directory

SHOP

Shopping A–Z

À LA MÈRE DE FAMILLE

lameredefamille.com

This original 18th-century grocery shop has shelves laden with imaginatively created chocolates, jams and unusual groceries. Beautifully packaged, these edible treats make great presents to take back home. There are ten stores around the city.

➕ H2 ✉ 33 35 rue du Faubourg Montmartre, 75009 ☎ 01 47 70 83 69 🕐 Mon–Sat 9.30–8, Sun 10–7.30 🚇 Le Peletier, Cadet

AGNÈS B

agnesb.eu

Agnès B's fashion is the epitome of young Parisian chic: sharply cut clothes with original details. French-born Agnès worked her way up from assistant fashion editor to own-name label, and her distinctive brand of clothes is still made in France.

➕ J4 ✉ 6 rue du Jour, 75001 ☎ 01 45 08 56 56 🕐 Mon–Fri 10.30–7.30, Sat 10–8 🚇 Les Halles

ARTAZART

artazart.com

Located on the banks of the Canal Saint-Martin, this bookshop specializes in design, architecture, photography and fashion. A small gallery shows work by up-and-coming artists.

➕ M7 ✉ 83 quai de Valmy, 75010 ☎ 01 40 40 24 03 🕐 Mon–Fri 10.30–7.30, Sat 11–7.30, Sun 1–7.30 🚇 Jacques Bonsergent, République

AU BAIN MARIE

aubainmarie.fr

Ceramic artist Aude Clément founded this now renowned emporium to sell her own

hand-crafted ranges of tableware and practical objets d'art. The impressive showroom now sells a specially chosen selection from other ceramic artists.

➕ G6 ✉ 56 rue de l'Université, 75007 ☎ 01 42 71 08 69 🕐 Tue–Sat 11–7 🚇 Solferino

AZZEDINE ALAÏA

alaia.fr

Alaïa, an artistic genius of the fashion world, is a Tunisian-born fashion designer with an eye for "feminine Hollywood" glamor, and the showroom is the place to come for his signature silhouette-hugging dresses.

➕ K6 ✉ 7 rue de Moussy, 75004 ☎ 01 42 72 30 69 🕐 Mon–Sat 10–7 🚇 Hôtel de Ville

BHV

bhv.fr

You can't buy shoes in this department store, but otherwise it's famous for having everything you'll ever need, from baby clothes to an electrical transformer. You can even get your watch battery replaced should you need to.

➕ K6 ✉ 52 rue de Rivoli, 75004 ☎ 09 77 40 14 00 🕐 Mon–Fri 9.30–8, Sat 9.30–8.30 Sun 11–7 🚇 Hôtel de Ville

SHOP

Most of the big-name designers are on rue du Faubourg Saint-Honoré and avenue Montaigne, but you'll also find women's high fashion on the place des Victoires (home to Kenzo and Victoire), the rue Étienne-Marcel and toward Les Halles. In the Marais, the best shopping runs between rue de Sévigné, rue des Rosiers, place des Vosges and side streets. In Saint-Germain, look along and off boulevard Saint-Germain, on rue de Grenelle and up boulevard Raspail.

LE BON MARCHÉ RIVE GAUCHE

lebonmarche.com

Classy goods abound in this Left Bank store. Don't miss the beauty shop on the ground floor or the excellent food hall, La Grande Épicerie, in an adjoining building, which stocks delicacies from all over the world.

➕ F7 ✉ 24 rue de Sèvres, 75007
☎ 01 44 39 80 00 🕐 Mon–Wed, Fri–Sat 10–8, Thu 10–8.45, Sun 11–8
🚇 Sèvres–Babylone

CARTIER

cartier.fr

This is the traditional Paris home of the exclusive jeweler, known the world over, selling contemporary and vintage jewelry, watches, leather goods and perfumes. There's another branch right around the corner on place Vendôme.

➕ G3 ✉ 13 rue de la Paix, 75002
☎ 01 58 18 23 00 🕐 Mon–Sat 11–7, Sun 11–6 🚇 Opéra

CHANEL

chanel.com

Chanel's fashion embodies Parisian style. Here, there is everything from fashion to jewelry, leather goods, watches, sunglasses, perfume and beauty products.

➕ D4 ✉ 51 avenue Montaigne, 75008
☎ 01 40 70 73 00 🕐 Mon–Sat 10–7, Sun 11–7 🚇 Franklin D. Roosevelt

CHRISTIAN LOUBOUTIN

christianlouboutin.com

A shoe fetishist's dream, Christian Louboutin is the place to go for exquisite women's shoes with glamor and extreme heels.

➕ H5 ✉ 19 rue Jean-Jacques Rousseau 75001 ☎ 0800 94 58 04 🕐 Mon–Sat 10.30–7 🚇 Louvre–Rivoli

DEHILLERIN

e-dehillerin.fr

Come here for all your top-end kitchen needs—copper pans, knives, bains-marie, sieves and much more.

➕ H4 ✉ 18–20 rue Coquillière, 75001
☎ 01 42 36 53 13 🕐 Mon 9–12.30, 2–6, Tue–Fri 9–7, Sat 9–6 🚇 Les Halles, Louvre–Rivoli

DETAILLE

detaille.com

This Paris beauty shop, which is more than 100 years old, was opened by the Countess de Presle, one of the first people in Paris to own a car. She created the store's best-selling antipollution face cream, Baume Automobile.

➕ G2 ✉ 10 rue Saint-Lazare, 75009
☎ 01 48 78 68 50 🕐 Tue–Sat 11–2, 3–7 🚇 Notre-Dame-de-Lorette

DIDIER LUDOT

didierludot.fr

Good-quality pre-owned vintage designer clothes (by the likes of

Chanel, Dior, Balmain, Givenchy and Lanvin) and classic Hermès handbags are sold at this shop in a picturesque location.

✚ H4 ✉ 20–24 Galerie Montpensier, 75001 ☎ 01 42 96 06 56 🕙 Mon–Sat 10.30–7 🚇 Palais-Royal–Musée du Louvre

DIOR

dior.com

Dior's historic headquarters sells everything from the ready-to-wear collection to menswear, jewelry and accessories. The store offers the current season's range, and includes classic evening wear.

✚ C4 ✉ 30 avenue Montaigne, 75008 ☎ 01 45 63 12 51 🕙 Mon–Sat 10–7, 🚇 Franklin D. Roosevelt

DIPTYQUE

diptyqueparis.fr

Diptyque sells the ultimate in crafted candles, in a choice of 48 exquisite scents. There's also a divine range of eau de cologne.

✚ J7 ✉ 34 boulevard Saint-Germain, 75005 ☎ 01 43 26 77 44 🕙 Mon–Sat 10.30–7.30 🚇 Maubert–Mutualité

DROUOT RICHELIEU

drouot.com

Paris's main auction rooms are where anything from a Persian carpet to a Louis XV commode may come under the hammer.

✚ H2 ✉ 9 rue Drouot, 75009 ☎ 01 48 00 20 20 🕙 Mon–Wed, Fri 11–6, Thu 11–9 (most auctions start at 2pm); closed Aug 🚇 Richelieu–Drouot

FAUCHON

fauchon.com

Paris's most renowned *épicerie* is a visual and gastronomic feast for foodies, complete with an excellent pâtisserie, a deli and a wine shop in imposing premises close to the Madeleine.

✚ F3 ✉ 30 place de la Madeleine, 75008 ☎ 01 70 39 38 02 🕙 Mon–Sat 10–8.30, boulangerie Mon–Sat 8–7 🚇 Madeleine

FORUM DES HALLES

forumdeshalles.com

Partially underground, this shopping complex is the biggest in central Paris and contains a few surprises—including a Muji store—among its predominantly mainstream fashion brands. The complex has also benefited from a multimillion-euro refit.

✚ J5 ✉ 1–7 rue Pierre-Lescot, 75001 ☎ 01 44 76 96 56 🕙 Mon–Sat 10–8.30, Sun 11–7 🚇 Châtelet-Les Halles

GALERIE CAPTIER

galeriecaptier.com

The antique Chinese and Japanese furniture (17th to 19th century) and beautiful old Japanese screens sold here have been chosen by owners Bernard and Sylvie Captier, who regularly travel to Asia to search out exotic and refined works of art.

Vintage fashion at Didier Ludot

G6 ✉ 33 rue de Beaune, 75007
☎ 01 42 61 00 57 🕐 Mon 2.30–7,
Tue–Sat 11–7 🚇 Rue du Bac

LA GALERIE FAYET

galerie-fayet.com

Owned for many years by the now-retired Mr Segas, this quirky shop selling antique walking canes is tucked into an attractive, historic 19th-century shopping arcade. The collection was expanded by the current owners to include a range of high-quality umbrellas.

H3 ✉ 34 passage Jouffroy, 75001
☎ 01 47 70 89 65 🕐 Tue–Fri 10.45–12.30, 1–7; Sat 10.30–12.30, 1–7 🚇 Grands Boulevards

GALERIE DE L'OPÉRA DE PARIS

This boutique-bookshop focuses on opera and choreography, with all the latest CDs and books, as well as a selection of postcards, posters and gifts. It's also the place to buy your opera glasses for the evening performance.

G3 ✉ Opéra Palais Garnier, rue Halévy, 75009 ☎ 01 40 01 17 82 🕐 Daily 10–6
🚇 Opéra

GOYARD

goyard.com

Founded in 1792 and in the same premises since 1834, Goyard manufactures and sells some of the world's finest luggage. Beautifully crafted, rugged and a classic statement of style, these trunks and bags are underground style icons.

F4 ✉ 233 rue Saint-Honoré, 75001
☎ 01 42 60 57 04 🕐 Mon–Sat 10–7
🚇 Concorde, Tuileries

LEMAIRE

lemaire.fr

Christophe Lemaire, once artistic director at Hermès, now puts his creative talent to his own avant-garde men's and women's ready-to-wear collection at this bijou boutique in the Marais.

L4 ✉ 28 rue de Poitou, 75003 ☎ 01 44 78 00 09 🕐 Mon 1–7, Tue–Sat 11–7.30 🚇 Filles du Calvaire

LIBRAIRIE DES ABBESSES

librairiedesabbesses.fr

In a city famed for its writers and novelists, independent bookshops are now a rarity, but this is a great little bookshop for those who read French or want to practice. It also sells beautiful art books.

c2 ✉ 30 rue Yvonne le Tac, 75018
☎ 01 46 06 84 30 🕐 Mon 11–8, Tue–Fri 9.30–8, Sat 10–8, Sun 12–8 🚇 Abbesses

LOUIS VUITTON

louisvuitton.com

The ultimate brand name on the Champs-Élysées and an essential store for all label-conscious visitors.

SHOP

Louis Vuitton began his business in the 1850s and the accessories are still synonymous with quality.

➕ C3 ✉ 101 avenue des Champs-Élysées, 75008 ☎ 01 53 57 52 00 🕒 Mon–Sat 10–8, Sun 11–8 🚇 George V

MARCHÉ BARBÈS

Come to this colorful market for ethnic wares, scarves, fruit, spices and vegetables. Shop where the locals shop for a taste of Parisian neighborhood banter.

➕ Off map at d2 ✉ Boulevard de la Chapelle, 75018 🕒 Wed 8–1, Sat 7–3 🚇 Barbès–Rochechouart

MARCHÉ AUX FLEURS

Housed in picturesque pavilions, this flower and plant market meets every horticultural need. You'll din thousands of pots on display, plus trees and shrubs.

➕ J6 ✉ Place Louis Lépine, 75004, Île de la Cité 🕒 Mon–Sat 8–7.30 (bird market on Sun) 🚇 Cité

MARCHÉ DE LA RUE LEPIC

It's up a steep hill but worth the effort to explore this atmospheric street, made famous in the film *Amélie* (2001). The best food shops are from the junction with rue des Abbesses down to boulevard de Clichy.

➕ b2 ✉ Rue Lepic and rue des Abbesses, 75018 🕒 Most shops open Tue–Sat 9–1, 4–7, Sun 9–1 🚇 Abbesses, Blanche

MARIAGE FRÈRES

mariagefreres.com
This teahouse, founded in 1854, offers a choice of hundreds of teas from all over the world, including a selection of exclusive house blends. The company also sells accessories like fine porcelain

Louis Vuitton on the Champs-Élysées

teapots and cups. There is also a restaurant on-site that serves lunch and afternoon tea.

➕ K6 ✉ 30 rue du Bourg-Tibourg, 75004 ☎ 01 42 72 28 11 🕒 Daily 10.30–7.30; tea room 12–7 🚇 Hôtel de Ville

MERCI

merci-merci.com
Shop with stylish Parisians at this concept store for an astonishing range of clothing, homewares and decor. There's a used bookstore and three casual eateries on site.

➕ M5 ✉ 111 boulevard Beaumarchais, 75003 ☎ 01 42 77 00 33 🕒 Daily 10–7.30 🚇 Saint-Sébastien Froissart

NAÏLA DE MONBRISON

naila-de-monbrison.com
If you are looking for an item of jewelry that isn't mainstream, this store stocks a great choice by a number of contemporary independent designers. The range runs the complete gamut of precious and semi-precious stones, metalwork and glass, and includes some extremely eye-catching pieces.

Flower market on the Île de la Cité

🔲 E5 ✉ 6 rue de Bourgogne, 75007
☎ 01 47 05 11 15 🕔 Mon–Sat 11–1.30,
2.30–7 🚇 Assemblée Nationale

PARIS SAINT-GERMAIN STORE
boutiquepsg.fr
Paris may be the city of romance,
but it is its world-famous soccer
team, Paris Saint-Germain (or PSG
as it is more popularly known),
that ignites the passions of Paris's
many soccer fans. This flagship
store sells a wide range of official
merchandise, including team
shirts, plus a selection of PSG-
related memorabilia.
🔲 D3 ✉ 27 avenue de Champs-Élysées,
75008 ☎ 0969 32 21 62 🕔 Mon–Sat
10–10, Sun 10–9 🚇 Franklin D. Roosevelt

PATRICK ROGER
patrickroger.com
Winner of the prestigious Meilleur
Ouvrier de France (Best Craftsman
in France) for chocolate products,
Patrick Roger is a sculptor of chocolate as well as a chocolate maker.
🔲 H7 ✉ 108 boulevard Saint-Germain,
75006 ☎ 01 43 29 38 42 🕔 Daily 10.30–
7.30 🚇 Odéon

PETIT BATEAU
petit-bateau.com
Every grown-up Parisienne has a
chic Petit Bateau T-shirt, a brand
known for its excellent quality and
fit. The company is also renowned
for its well-made everyday baby
and children's collections.
🔲 b2 ✉ 50 rue des Abbesses, 75018
☎ 01 42 52 81 76 🕔 Mon–Sat 11–7
🚇 Abbesses

PIERRE HERMÉ
pierreherme.com
The couture pastries are as
visually stunning as they are
mouthwatering and the gold-leaf
ornamented chocolate cake is
legendary. You could also take
home a delightfully presented box
of macaroons as a gift.
🔲 G7 ✉ 72 rue Bonaparte, 75006
☎ 01 43 54 47 77 🕔 Daily 9–8
🚇 Saint-Sulpice, Mabillon

RUE MOUFFETARD
Visit this tourist classic straggling
down a narrow, hilly street, for a
wonderful array of shops and stalls
selling fruit and veg, *charcuterie*
and aromatic cheeses. There are
good café stops en route.
🔲 J9 ✉ Rue Mouffetard, 75005 🕔 Daily,
but some shops and stalls close Sun–Mon
🚇 Monge

LE SEPT CINQ
sept-cinq.com
For stylish clothing or jewelry
by local creatives, head to this
concept store. Everything on sale
is by Parisian designers, including
socks by Royalties and espadrilles
by Barre Paris.
🔲 B3 ✉ 54 rue Notre-Dame-de-Lorette,
75009 ☎ 09 83 55 05 95 🕔 Mon–Sat
11–8 🚇 Pigalle

SHAKESPEARE AND COMPANY

shakespeareandcompany.com

Opened in 1951, this English-language bookstore quickly became a magnet for ex-pat writers and wannabe literary characters. Allen Ginsberg and Henry Miller were just two of the literary giants who came here to browse and chat.

🔢 J7 ✉ 37 rue de la Bûcherie, 75005 ☎ 01 43 25 40 93 🕐 Mon–Sat 10–10, Sun 12.30–8 🚇 Saint-Michel

SI TU VEUX

situveuxjouer.com

The perfect toy shop, Si Tu Veux sells affordable toys, games and dressing-up clothes and other accessories. There's a good range of options for creative play for all ages, excellent old-style wooden toys and a separate section devoted to teddy bears.

🔢 H4 ✉ 68 Galerie Vivienne, 75002 ☎ 01 42 60 59 97 🕐 Mon–Sat 10.30–7 🚇 Bourse

STOHRER

stohrer.fr

When the Polish wife of King Louis XV moved into Versailles palace she brought her *patissier*, Nicolas Stohrer, with her. Five years later he opened this shop and here, it is said, the delectable rum baba was invented.

🔢 J4 ✉ 51 rue Montorgueil, 75002 ☎ 01 40 33 38 20 🕐 Daily 7.30am–8.30pm 🚇 Les Halles

VANESSA BRUNO

vanessabruno.com

This designer's practical, easy-to-wear women's clothing has won her a loyal following. The 1960s- and '70s-inspired designs are renowned for their stylish flair. The "cabas" leather bag quickly become a classic must-have item after its launch.

🔢 L5 ✉ 100 rue Vieille-du-Temple, 75003 ☎ 01 42 77 19 41 🕐 Mon 12.30–7.30, Tue–Sat 10.30–7.30, Sun 2–7 🚇 Filles du Calvaire

WOLFORD

wolfordshop.fr

Purveyors of high-class hosiery, support garments and swimwear, Wolford is the ideal place to find the perfect foundation for your prêt-a-porter outfits, with a high quality that Parisians will pay a premium for.

🔢 C3 ✉ 39 rue Marbeuf, 75008 ☎ 01 42 25 09 09 🕐 Mon 11–7, Tue–Sat 10–7 🚇 Franklin D. Roosevelt

ZADIG & VOLTAIRE

zadig-et-voltaire.com

There's a youthful edge to the men's and womenswear at this Left Bank outpost of the internationally successful fashion house founded by Frenchman Thierry Gillier, son of the founder of the Lacoste empire.

🔢 G6 ✉ 10 rue de Grenelle, 75005 ☎ 01 43 20 79 63 🕐 Mon–Sat 10.30–7 🚇 Saint-Germain-des-Prés

SHOP

BOUTIQUING

The streets around the Abbesses Métro station offer a treasure trove of quirky independent clothing, accessories and gift boutiques. For fabulous food shops head down the rue des Abbesses and turn left on rue Lepic. Another wonderful food shopping area in Montmartre is the stretch of rue des Martyrs that descends below the boulevard de Clichy.

Entertainment

Once you've done with sightseeing for the day, you'll find lots of other great things to do with your time in this chapter, even if all you want to do is relax with a drink. In this section, establishments are listed alphabetically.

ENTERTAINMENT

Introduction

The heart of Paris has a special beauty at night, and an electric atmosphere. Boulevards, great monuments and historic buildings are dazzlingly illuminated. The Champs-Élysées, place de la Concorde and the Louvre make a magnificent spectacle of lights against the night sky. The soaring Eiffel Tower, shining like gold and glittering for five minutes every hour, and the silvery white of the Sacré-Cœur Basilica are majestic landmarks.

Nightlife by Area

In a city as big as Paris there is no single focus for nightlife, and where you go will depend on what you are looking for. Small theaters and jazz clubs still dot the Left Bank, and there are more jazz clubs around Châtelet and Les Halles. While there's a chic and expensive feel to many of the bars and clubs in the west, between Étoile and Opéra, Montmartre, Pigalle and Clichy offer nightlife of an altogether more raffish kind. However, their many sex shops and strip joints are interspersed with mainstream discos and some of the city's best live music venues, so it's not an area to be written off as too sleazy. The eastern *arrondissements* have some of the most interesting and fashionable nightlife, from the Marais' LGBTQ+ scene and

---

AN EVENING STROLL

Start at Châtelet and walk toward the Louvre along the embankment opposite the illuminated Conciergerie, the Monnaie and the Institut de France. At the Louvre make a detour into the magnificently lit Cour Carrée. Return to the river, cross the Pont des Arts, then walk back along the opposite bank, with views north to the stately Samaritaine and the Palais de Justice on the Île de la Cité. Continue toward Saint-Michel, then cross over to Notre-Dame and make your way around the north side of the island for good views.

Clockwise from top: Evening view of the domed Institut de France, with the Pont des Arts in the foreground; the Opéra Bastille; cafés, bars and clubs line the streets of

branché (trendy) café society to the scuffed boho chic of lively rue Oberkampf.

Glamorous Fun
There's a sense of excitement, anticipation and enjoyment in Paris. In addition to glamorous cabarets, there are world-class ballet, concert and opera venues, nightclubs, discos, café-theaters and atmospheric bars with live music. Although the Métro is closed from 1.15am (2.15 Friday and Saturday) to 5.30am, plenty of taxis run at night, as well as the Noctilien buses (ratp.fr).

Clubbing Paris Style
Dressing up—not down—is still often the rule when you go dancing in Paris, and if your clothes don't pass muster you may not get past the door at some clubs. Drinks prices can be steep but the price of entry often includes a *conso* (free drink).

Added Magic
A boat trip along the Seine between the illuminated buildings adds extra magic, and *bateaux mouches* run every evening until 10.30 (9.20 in winter). For experienced in-line skaters a high-speed three-hour skating tour of Paris takes place every Friday at 9.30pm (see pari-roller.com for details).

LGBTQ+ PARIS
As befits a 21st-century, cosmopolitan city that had an openly gay mayor—Bertrand Delanoë—from 2001 to 2014, Paris is a welcoming place for LGBTQ+ visitors, particularly in the fashionable Marais district, where the list of entertainment venues stretches beyond the established confines of the official scene. The hugely popular Open Café (✉ 17 rue des Archives ☎ 01 42 72 26 18, opencafe.fr) and slick Raidd (✉ 23 rue du Temple ☎ 01 44 77 04 88) are two of the area's best places to see and be seen in.

Montmartre; enjoying a night out; a delightful evening scene in Paris; there are plenty of clubs to choose from; the famous Moulin Rouge

ENTERTAINMENT

Directory

AROUND THE TOUR EIFFEL
Clubs
Le Club

LATIN QUARTER, ST-GERMAIN AND ISLANDS
Bars
Caveau de la Huchette
Compagnie des Vins Surnaturels
Cinemas
Le Champo
Lucernaire/Centre national
 d'Art et d'Essai
Studio Galande
Classical Music
Musée de Cluny – Musée national
 du Moyen-Âge
Theaters
Théâtre de la Huchette

MARAIS AND BASTILLE
Cinemas
Forum des Images
Clubs
Duc des Lombards
Favela Chic
La Java
Sunset-Sunside
Opera
Opéra Bastille
Theater/Dance
Théâtre du Châtelet
Théâtre de la Ville

LOUVRE AND CHAMPS-ÉLYSÉES
Bars
Le Bar du Bristol
Barramundi
Delaville
Harry's New York Bar
Cinemas
Le Balzac
Classical Music
Auditorium du Louvre
Clubs
Club l'Arc
Shows
Le Crazy Horse
Theaters
Comédie Française/Salle Richelieu

MONTMARTRE
Cinemas
Studio 28
Clubs
Michou
Contemporary Music
La Boule Noire/La Cigale
Le Bus Palladium
Divan du Monde
Shows
Moulin Rouge

FARTHER AFIELD
Classical Music
Philharmonie de Paris

ENTERTAINMENT

Entertainment A–Z

AUDITORIUM DU LOUVRE

louvre.fr

High-quality lunchtime, afternoon, teatime and evening concerts are held in this 450-seat auditorium beneath the Louvre's pyramid. Each season is based on a theme and features soloists and ensembles performing a range of pieces, from contemporary and popular classics to music that's been commissioned by the museum.

➕ G5 ✉ Musée du Louvre (entrance by the pyramid), 75001 ☎ 01 40 20 55 50 🚇 Palais-Royal

LE BALZAC

cinemabalzac.com

Le Balzac is famous for its screenings of American independent films (in the original language) and for the debates that often follow. Concerts are held before Saturday evening screenings. There's also a bar on site.

➕ B3 ✉ 1 rue Balzac, 75008 ☎ 01 45 61 02 53 🚇 George V, Charles de Gaulle–Étoile

LE BAR DU BRISTOL

lebristolparis.com

Set in the high-class Le Bristol hotel, this equally elegant bar is one of the top cocktail venues in the city, whose inventive mixologist has created a menu of classic and new drinks. There are DJ sessions Tuesday to Saturday.

➕ E3 ✉ 112 rue du Faubourg Saint-Honoré, 75008 ☎ 01 53 43 43 00 🕐 Daily 5.30pm–2am 🚇 Miromesnil

BARRAMUNDI

barramundi.fr

Barramundi draws a fashionable crowd with its world music, bar, lounge and eclectic restaurant. This is one of Paris's top chill-out spots.

➕ H3 ✉ 3 rue Taitbout, 75009 ☎ 01 47 70 21 21 🕐 Mon–Fri 12–3.30pm, 6.30pm–2am, Sat 7pm–5am 🚇 Richelieu–Drouot, Chaussée d'Antin

LA BOULE NOIRE/LA CIGALE

lacigale.fr

Famous names have played at the diminutive La Boule Noire, including Franz Ferdinand, Jamie Cullum and Metallica. It's linked to a former theater, La Cigale, a listed historic monument, and hosts musicals, rock and pop, and music festivals.

➕ c2 ✉ 120 boulevard Rochechouart, 75018 ☎ 01 49 25 89 99 🚇 Pigalle, Anvers

LE BUS PALLADIUM

buspalladium.com

An iconic rock venue since the 1960s, when Mick Jagger came to relax, it still proudly reverberates to a heavy beat, with live bands and DJ sets. There's a cool bar even if the music isn't to your taste.

➕ G1 ✉ 6 rue Pierre Fontaine, 75009 ☎ 01 45 26 80 35 🕐 Tue–Thu 9pm–2am, Fri–Sat 9pm–3am 🚇 Pigalle

CAVEAU DE LA HUCHETTE

caveaudelahuchette.fr

Still going strong after 60 years, having hosted many of the great

Numerous classical music concerts are held in churches—try Saint-Eustache, Saint-Germain-des-Prés, Saint-Julien-le-Pauvre, Saint-Louis-en-l'Île, Saint-Roch and Saint-Séverin (ampconcerts.com). Seats are reasonably priced and the quality of music is sometimes very high. From May to September free concerts are held in parks. Schedules are available at the Office du Tourisme or the Hôtel de Ville.

names in jazz, this basement bar hosts live jazz and dancing.

➕ J7 ✉ 5 rue de la Huchette, 75005 ☎ 01 43 26 65 05 🕐 Daily from 9.30pm 🚇 Saint-Michel

LE CHAMPO

lechampo.com

Come here for cult classics, with retrospectives of famous directors such as the Marx Brothers, Claude Chabrol and Jacques Tati. Films are in the original language.

➕ J7 ✉ 51 rue des Écoles, 75015 ☎ 01 43 29 79 04 🕐 Daily, times vary 🚇 Saint-Michel, Odéon, Cluny–La Sorbonne

LE CLUB

the-club.fr

Renowned mixologists Seb and Olivier create some of Paris's best cocktails at their bar designed by stylist Philippe Modal. There's a long cocktail menu, and they'll be happy to oblige if you request something unique.

➕ D5 ✉ 24 rue Surcouf, 75007 ☎ 01 45 50 31 54 🕐 Mon–Sat 4pm–2am 🚇 Invalides

CLUB L'ARC

larc-paris.com

This long-standing favorite has been renovated by American rock star Lenny Kravitz. It's one of the most fashionable places in town.

➕ B2 ✉ 12 rue de Presbourg, 75016 ☎ 06 09 86 00 15 🕐 Thu–Sat midnight–5am 🚇 Charles de Gaulle–Étoile

COMÉDIE FRANÇAISE/ SALLE RICHELIEU

comedie-francaise.fr

The Comédie Française, home to France's most prestigious troupe of actors, was founded by Louis XIV in 1680. Today, the repertoire is made up of the classics, including works by Shakespeare, Molière and Victor Hugo, and a few modern pieces.

➕ G4 ✉ 1 place Colette, 75001 ☎ 01 44 58 04 00 🕐 Performances daily, times vary, some matinées Sat, Sun 🚇 Palais-Royal–Musée du Louvre

COMPAGNIE DES VINS SURNATURELS

compagniedesvinssurnaturels.com

Enjoy some of France's finest wines by the glass in this elegant lounge. Parisians arrive here after work for pre-dinner drinks or come later in the evening to savor some of the country's most prestigious labels.

➕ H7 ✉ 7 rue Lobineau, 75006 ☎ 09 54 90 20 20 🕐 Daily 6pm–2am 🚇 Mabillon

LE CRAZY HORSE

lecrazyhorseparis.com

This world-renowned burlesque show has been wowing audiences with its naughty but humorous routines, gorgeous dancers and dazzling, albeit scanty, costumes by top designers since 1951.

➕ C4 ✉ 12 avenue George V, 75008 ☎ 01 47 23 32 32 🕐 Shows: Sun–Fri

8 and 11, Sat 7, 9.30 and midnight
🚇 George V, Alma–Marceau

DELAVILLE
delavilleparis.com

Opened in the 1860s, Delaville embraces the zeitgeist by transforming itself from café and tea bar by day into club and cabaret as night falls. It has a vibe that harks back to the Josephine Baker era with DJ sets and dancers.
➕ J3 ✉ 34–36 boulevard Bonne Nouvelle, 75010 ☎ 01 48 24 48 09 🕐 Daily 8.30am–2am 🚇 Bonne Nouvelle

DIVAN DU MONDE
divandumonde.com

Devoted to French music, this former brothel and club is now one of the latest Francophone venues. The regular program ranges from live cabaret with Madame Arthur to French dance and club music sessions.
➕ C3 ✉ 75 rue des Martyrs, 75018 ☎ 07 68 78 68 01 🕐 Thu–Sun midnight–6am 🚇 Pigalle

DUC DES LOMBARDS
ducdeslombards.com

Prestigious jazz musicians regularly play in this Les Halles club. Late night Friday and Saturday there's free entry for a free-form jam session that carries on until the early hours.
➕ J5 ✉ 42 rue des Lombards, 75001 ☎ 01 42 33 22 88 🕐 Closed Sun 🚇 Châtelet

FAVELA CHIC
favelachic.com

The sounds, flavors and vibrant style of urban Brazil pound out in this club, with a restaurant, live bands and DJs. It includes a pop-up gallery and a quirky, chill-out lounge zone.
➕ M3 ✉ 18 rue du Faubourg du Temple, 75011 ☎ 01 40 21 38 14 🕐 Tue–Thu 7.30pm–2am, Fri–Sat 7.30pm–5am 🚇 Pigalle

FORUM DES IMAGES
forumdesimages.fr

Films or documentaries shot in or connected with Paris and movie classics are screened here, along with independent documentaries from around the world. A day pass admits you to all screenings. Visit the website for other venues around the city.
➕ J5 ✉ 2 rue du Cinéma, Port Saint-Eustache, Forum des Halles, 75001 ☎ 01 44 76 63 00 🕐 Tue, Thu 5–9, Wed 1–9, Fri 4–9, Sat–Sun 10.30am–9pm 🚇 Les Halles, Châtelet

HARRY'S NEW YORK BAR
harrysbar.fr

Harry's in New York was dismantled and shipped lock, stock and barrel to Paris just before World War I. It's famous for having hundreds of cocktails.
➕ G3 ✉ 5 rue Daunou, 75002 ☎ 01 42 61 71 14 🕐 Mon–Sat noon–2am, Sun 4pm–1am 🚇 Opéra

POOLS AND HORSES

Paris's municipal swimming pools have complicated opening hours largely geared to schoolchildren. Phone to check for public hours and avoid Wednesday and Saturday, popular times for children off school. If horse-racing is your passion, don't miss the harness-racing at Vincennes (letrot.com), with its brilliant flashes of color-coordinated horses and jockeys. Check the racing newspaper *Paris-Turf* (paris-turf.com) for race schedules.

LA JAVA

la-java.fr

Set in the basement of an Art Deco building, La Java has been open since the 1920s and has seen performances by such illustrious artists as Édith Piaf and Django Reinhardt. Today the tiny venue concentrates on contemporary urban music and has a popular LGBTQ+ following.

🏛 Off map at M3 ✉ 105 rue du Faubourg du Temple 75010 ☎ 01 42 02 20 52 🕐 Thu–Sun 7pm–2am 🚇 Belleville

LUCERNAIRE/CENTRE NATIONAL D'ART ET D'ESSAI

lucernaire.fr

This complex of three cinemas, an art gallery, bar, restaurant and three theaters stages a wide variety of plays. Housed in a former factory, it attracts top French actors.

🏛 G8 ✉ 53 rue Notre-Dame-des-Champs, 75006 ☎ 01 45 44 57 34 🚇 Vavin, Notre-Dame-des-Champs

MICHOU

michou.com

A familiar sight in the district, Michou is always dressed in electric-blue suits and big eyeglasses. The drag show in this venerable club is still going strong.

BEAUTIFUL PEOPLE

The clubs around the Champs-Élysées tend to attract VIPs, celebrities and a generally well-heeled crowd. Clubs usually don't open until 11pm or midnight, and often stay open until dawn. For a more laid-back, arty bar scene, go to the bar-lined rue Oberkampf or the Canal Saint-Martin area. The Marais district is also packed with bars, many of them LGBTQ+ or mixed.

🏛 C2 ✉ 80 rue des Martyrs, 75018 ☎ 01 46 06 16 04 🕐 Nightly dinner 8.30pm, show 10.30pm 🚇 Pigalle

MOULIN ROUGE

moulinrouge.fr

The Red Windmill, made famous by Toulouse-Lautrec, opened in 1889 when audiences flocked to ogle at the dancers performing the cancan. These days the shows are still as spectacular but are more entertaining than scandalous.

🏛 b2 ✉ 82 boulevard de Clichy, 75018 ☎ 01 53 09 82 82 🕐 Nightly dinner and show 7pm; show only 9 and 11pm; see website for matinee performances 🚇 Blanche

MUSÉE DE CLUNY – MUSÉE-NATIONAL DU MOYEN-ÂGE

musee-moyenage.fr

This medieval mansion is home to a museum devoted to the Middle Ages (▷ 30–31), but it also hosts classical and chamber music concerts. Most appropriate is the medieval music.

🏛 J7 ✉ 6 place Paul-Painlevé, 75005 ☎ 01 53 73 78 16 🕐 Free concerts of medieval music: times vary 🚇 Cluny–La Sorbonne

OPÉRA BASTILLE

operadeparis.fr

The famous opera house towers over place de la Bastille and boasts five movable stages. Performances include opera, operettas, recitals, ballet, dance and theater.

🏛 M7 ✉ 130 rue de Lyon, 75012 ☎ 08 92 89 90 90 🚇 Bastille

PHILHARMONIE DE PARIS

philharmoniedeparis.fr

The city's spectacular, contemporary 1,500-seat venue is home to the

Orchestre de Paris and offers a rich program of solo artists, classical and rock concerts, family events and music workshops.

🔲 Off map at M1 ✉ 221 avenue Jean Jaurès, Parc de la Villette, 75019 ☎ 01 44 84 44 84 🚇 Porte de Pintin

STUDIO 28

cinema-studio28.fr

Studio 28 is a stylish cinema, where new releases in the original language change every day or two, and French classics are screened every month. It has its own little bar and garden where you can mingle with like-minded film aficionados if you want.

🔲 b2 ✉ 10 rue Tholozé, 75018 ☎ 01 46 06 36 07 🕐 Daily 3–9pm (start of last showing) 🚇 Abbesses, Blanche

STUDIO GALANDE

studiogalande.fr

Cult movie *The Rocky Horror Picture Show* is shown here every Friday and Saturday at 10pm, if you want to sing along. The rest of the week screenings range from art films to cartoons.

🔲 J7 ✉ 42 rue Galande, 75005 ☎ 01 43 54 72 71 🕐 Screenings daily from noon 🚇 Saint-Michel, Maubert–Mutualité, Cluny

SUNSET-SUNSIDE

sunset-sunside.com

Opened in 1984 as a venue for jazz of all descriptions, this club has evolved over the years into two jazz clubs: the Sunset offers a range of electric jazz and world music concerts, while the Sunside concentrates on acoustic jazz.

🔲 J5 ✉ 60 rue des Lombards, 75001 ☎ 01 40 26 46 60 🕐 Live performances daily 8.30pm or 9pm 🚇 Châtelet

THÉÂTRE DU CHÂTELET

chatelet-theatre.com

The Théâtre du Châtelet hosts a varied schedule of opera, symphonic music and dance, as well as popular Sunday morning concerts. It seats 2,500 people.

🔲 J6 ✉ 2 rue Edouard Colonne, 75001 ☎ 01 40 28 28 28 🕐 Check website calendar 🚇 Châtelet

THÉÂTRE DE LA HUCHETTE

theatre-huchette.com

Two of Ionesco's masterpieces, *La Cantatrice Chauve* (The Bald Soprano) and *La Leçon* (The Lesson), have been performed here five days a week for over 50 years. It's an intimate venue with room for just 85 people.

🔲 J7 ✉ 23 rue de la Huchette, 75005 ☎ 01 43 26 38 99 🕐 Tue–Sat 7pm and 8pm 🚇 Saint-Michel

THÉÂTRE DE LA VILLE

theatredelaville-paris.com

This modern venue showcases an adventurous program of avant-garde music, classical pieces, contemporary dance and plays, which include well-directed works by Shakespeare and Marlowe.

🔲 J6 ✉ 1 avenue Gabriel, 75004 ☎ 01 42 74 22 77 🕐 Performance times vary 🚇 Châtelet

Eat

There are places to eat across the city to suit all tastes and budgets. In this section, establishments are listed alphabetically.

EAT

Introduction

French cuisine is world renowned and Paris has a wealth of choice, from the best haute cuisine to restaurants concentrating on regional specialties. From established chefs to up-and-coming stars, the talent here is some of the finest on the planet.

The Best of the Best

The standard for the top and most innovative restaurants—the Michelin star—is the epitome of gastronomic excellence. Three stars is the ultimate. Book in advance and dress smartly at these addresses.

Eat Like a Parisian

Many restaurants serve a reasonably priced *menu du jour* (daily menu) of two or three courses with a glass of wine. The set-price lunch menu of fine-dining places is an opportunity to try good French cuisine on a budget.

What's in a Name?

Restaurants have higher prices than brasseries or bistros but will often have a refined setting, elegant cuisine and good wine list. Bistros have a short and often seasonal or daily menu, while brasseries serve French staples such as steaks, salads and seafood. Cafés and bars serve tea, coffee, cold drinks, snacks and sandwiches. *Salons de thé* (tearooms) are becoming popular and serve cakes and patisseries.

OPENING TIMES

Most restaurants and bistros keep strict serving times. Restaurants open at 12, close at 2.30, then reopen at 7.30 or 8. Brasseries and cafés open through the afternoon. Most Parisians take an hour for lunch and eat in the staff canteen or local bistro. The evening meal is usually eaten *en famille* between 8 and 9pm. Restaurants stop taking orders between 10 and 11pm. To eat later, try the Les Halles area or a brasserie. Some places close on weekends, in July and August, and in February.

From top: A table with a view at Le Jules Verne restaurant, Tour Eiffel; stopping for coffee; blackboard menu; a colorful dish at Guy Savoy's restaurant

EAT

Directory

AROUND THE TOUR EIFFEL
Asian
Benkay
French-Bistro
L'Affriolé
Bistrotters
French-Brasserie
Brasserie Thoumieux
French-Elegant
Le Jules Verne
French-Regional
L'Ami Jean

LATIN QUARTER, ST-GERMAIN AND ISLANDS
Asian
Desi Road
French-Bistro
Café Saint-Régis
Le Comptoir
Les Papilles
Le Petit Saint-Benoît
Ze Kitchen Galerie
French-Brasserie
Alcazar
La Coupole
French-Elegant
Guy Savoy
La Tour d'Argent

MARAIS AND BASTILLE
French-Bistro
L'Ange 20
Au Pied de Cochon
Bistrot Paul Bert
Chez Paul
Monjul
Pramil
Restaurant Frenchie
Tannat
French-Brasserie
Bofinger

French-Regional
Benoit
Breizh Café
Kosher
L'As du Fallafel
North African
404

LOUVRE AND CHAMPS-ÉLYSÉES
Café/Crêperie
Midi 12
French-Bistro
L'Avenue
Café Marly
French-Elegant
Le Céladon
Epicure
Taillevent
French-Regional
Carré des Feuillants
Fusion
6 New York

MONTMARTRE
French-Bistro
Au Virage Lepic
Le Progrès
Seb'on
French-Regional
Au Clair de la Lune
Italian/Mediterranean
Pink Mamma
Organic
Rose Bakery

FARTHER AFIELD
French-Bistro
La Petite Ardoise
French-Elegant
Gordon Ramsay au Trianon
Septime

Eating A–Z

6 NEW YORK €€

6newyork.fr

For beautiful contemporary decor and fusion food, head for 6 New York. Chef and owner Jerome Gangneux, who hails from Normandy, cooks with a lightness of touch that allows the fresh ingredients to reveal their flavors.

🔲 B5 ✉ 6 avenue de New York, 75016 ☎ 01 40 70 03 30 🕐 Mon–Fri lunch, dinner, Sat dinner 🚇 Alma–Marceau

404 €–€€

404-resto.com

This family-run restaurant serves excellent North African cuisine. Beautifully styled, it's like stepping into an Arab souk, with colorful ceramics, fine basketry and carpets festooning the walls. The dining room is part of an atmospheric 16th-century building.

🔲 K4 ✉ 69 rue des Gravilliers, 75003 ☎ 01 42 74 57 81 🕐 Daily lunch, dinner 🚇 Arts et Métiers

L'AFFRIOLÉ €–€€

laffriole.fr

This great-value nouveau bistro provides friendly service and classic French dishes. All wines are available by the glass, which is rare in Paris.

🔲 C5 ✉ 17 rue Malar, 75007 ☎ 01 85 15 23 93 🕐 Tue–Sat lunch, dinner 🚇 La Tour Maubourg, Pont de l'Alma, Invalides

ALCAZAR €€

alcazar.fr

One of the city's first modern bistros, Alcazar remains a city favorite after a total renovation. Michel Besmond oversees a selection of freshly prepared adventurous dishes, served in the eclectically styled yet relaxed dining room.

🔲 H6 ✉ 62 rue Mazarine, 75006 ☎ 01 53 10 19 99 🕐 Daily lunch, dinner 🚇 Odéon

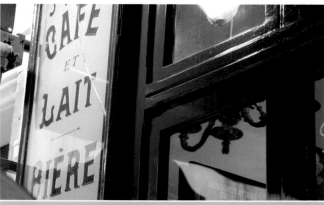

Coffees and beers in the Marais district

EAT

144

L'AMI JEAN €€–€€€

lamijean.fr

Owned by chef Stéphane Jego, an apprentice of pioneer Yves Camdeborde, this friendly restaurant serves traditional Basque dishes of beef and seafood with a contemporary slant and enhanced by fine wines.

➕ C5 ✉ 27 rue Malar, 75007 ☎ 01 47 05 86 89 🕐 Tue–Sat lunch, dinner 🚇 Pont de l'Alma, La Tour Maubourg, Invalides

L'ANGE 20 €€

lange20.com

The team keep their menu very simple, with each course (a choice of two or three dishes) at a set price. The menu features fresh French ingredients served with a modern twist and always elegantly executed.

➕ K5 ✉ 44 rue des Tournelles, 75004 ☎ 01 49 96 58 39 🕐 Wed–Sun lunch, dinner 🚇 Bastille

L'AS DU FALLAFEL €

This kosher restaurant has a cult following among visitors and Marais locals alike for its falafel and low prices. You'll probably have to wait in line, but it will be worth it. There is also a take-out menu.

➕ L6 ✉ 34 rue des Rosiers, 75007 ☎ 01 48 87 63 60 🕐 Sun–Thu 12–12, Fri lunch only 🚇 Saint-Paul

AU CLAIR DE LA LUNE €€

clairedelalune.fr

Classic French cuisine is served in this comfortable, welcoming inn-style restaurant just off the place du Tertre. It is run by two brothers and is popular with locals.

➕ C1 ✉ 9 rue Poulbot, 75018 ☎ 01 42 58 97 03 🕐 Daily lunch, dinner 🚇 Abbesses

AU PIED DE COCHON €€

pieddecochon.com

Pigs' trotters feature at this Parisian institution, along with seafood and sublime French onion soup, served in elegant surroundings. It attracts Parisians and tourists alike and is extremely popular with the late-night set.

➕ J4 ✉ 6 rue Coquillère, 75001 ☎ 01 40 13 77 00 🕐 Daily 24 hours 🚇 Les Halles

AU VIRAGE LEPIC €–€€

This welcoming bistro is well known for its tasty meat-based main courses and delicious puddings, complemented by a great wine list. In summer, you can sit outside.

➕ b1 ✉ 61 rue Lepic, 75018 ☎ 01 42 52 46 79 🕐 Wed–Mon dinner 🚇 Blanche, Abbesses

L'AVENUE €€

avenue-restaurant.com

The terrace of this long-standing café is perfect for people watching in one of the city's most upscale districts. The menu features typical bistro fare.

➕ C4 ✉ 41 avenue Montaigne, 75008 ☎ 01 40 70 14 91 🕐 Daily 8am–2am 🚇 Franklin D. Roosevelt

BENKAY €€

restaurant-benkay.com

Dine here on modern Japanese food and enjoy the panoramic views from the fourth floor of the Novotel Paris Tour Eiffel. Choose from a full-service sushi bar, a *washoku* traditional Japanese menu, and a showy *teppanyaki* station.

➕ A7 ✉ 61 quai de Grenelle, 75015 ☎ 01 40 58 21 26 🕐 Daily lunch, dinner 🚇 Bir-Hakeim

EAT

BENOIT €€–€€€

benoit-paris.com

This long-standing bistro serving classic regional dishes is owned by renowned chef Alain Ducasse. The dining room has an elegant period interior, matched by the food that is served by knowledgeable staff. Reserve ahead.

➕ J6 ✉ 20 rue Saint-Martin, 75004 ☎ 01 42 72 25 76 🕐 Daily lunch, dinner 🚇 Hôtel de Ville, Châtelet-Les Halles

BISTROT PAUL BERT €€

One of the last old-style bistros, Bistrot Paul Bert has a loyal clientele that comes back for its generous portions, the best steak in town, and a cheese plate that takes you on a dairy tour of France.

➕ Off map ✉ 18 rue Paul Bert, 75011 🕐 01 43 72 24 01 🕐 Tue–Sat lunch, dinner 🚇 Faidherbe–Chaligny

BISTROTTERS €

bistrotters.com

A small culinary team brings the flavors of the world to French ingredients in a menu that changes with the seasons. There's a wine shop on site where you can stock up on the bottles you enjoyed over dinner.

➕ Off map ✉ 9 rue Decrès, 75014 ☎ 01 45 45 58 59 🕐 Daily lunch, dinner 🚇 Plaisance

BOFINGER €€

bofingerparis.com

Claiming to be the oldest brasserie in Paris (1864), Bofinger adheres strongly to the traditional brasserie menu and serves seafood, *choucroute* and steaks, plus the ubiquitous onion soup. The refined interior is period-perfect art nouveau in style.

➕ M6 ✉ 5 rue de la Bastille, 75004 ☎ 01 42 72 87 82 🕐 Daily lunch, dinner 🚇 Bastille

BRASSERIE THOUMIEUX €€

thoumieux.com

Established in 1923, Thoumieux's mirrored walls and red velvet seats hark back to a classic era. Expect hearty *cassoulet* (sausage and bean casserole) and duck dishes. Upstairs is the pricey fine-dining Restaurant Sylvestre.

➕ D5 ✉ 79 rue Saint-Dominique, 75007 ☎ 01 47 05 79 00 🕐 Daily lunch, dinner 🚇 Invalides

BREIZH CAFÉ €

breizhcafe.com

The Breton *crêpe* (pancake) reaches exalted heights of finesse here, with sweet and savory options. Try something unusual, such as a *crêpe* with oysters. It's also worth a visit to choose from over 30 ciders—a specialty of the French region of Brittany.

➕ L5 ✉ 109 rue Vieille-du-Temple, 75003 ☎ 01 47 05 79 00 🕐 Daily lunch, dinner 🚇 Filles du Calvaire

CAFÉ MARLY €€

cafe-marly.com

This café-restaurant in the Louvre must have one of the best terraces in the world, with its exceptional view of architect I.M. Pei's stunning

EAT

The French are famous for their crusty bread

glass pyramid framing the opposite wing of the museum. The food on offer here is good and the service is friendly.

🔲 G5 ✉ 93 rue de Rivoli, 75001 ☎ 01 49 26 06 60 🕐 Daily 8am–2am (last orders midnight) 🚇 Palais-Royal–Musée du Louvre

CAFÉ SAINT RÉGIS €–€€

cafesaintregisparis.com

The menu of this traditional French café melds Gallic classics with contemporary fashion, with *croque monsieur* sitting side by side with tapas sardines. Enjoy the atmosphere of île Saint-Louis from the terrace on a balmy summer evening.

🔲 K7 ✉ rue Jean du Bellay, Île Saint-Louis, 75004 ☎ 01 43 54 59 41 🕐 Daily 6am–2am 🚇 Pont Marie, Sully Morland

CARRÉ DES FEUILLANTS €€€

carredesfeuillants.fr

You'll find an elegant setting for Alain Dutournier's evocation of the cooking of his native Gascony. He uses the best ingredients to wonderful effect, earning a high reputation for his restaurant.

🔲 F4 ✉ 14 rue de Castiglione, 75001 ☎ 01 42 86 82 82 🕐 Mon–Fri lunch, dinner. Closed Aug 🚇 Tuileries

LE CÉLADON €€–€€€

leceladon.com

Opened in 2019 after renovations and serving interesting variations on French classics, Le Céladon offers a good-value weekday lunch menu that is ideal for anyone wanting to explore French haute-cuisine. Menus feature creative dishes using seasonal fruit and vegetables. It opens as Le Petit Céladon on Saturdays.

🔲 G3 ✉ Hôtel Westminster, 15 rue Daunou, 75002 ☎ 01 47 03 40 42 🕐 Mon–Sat lunch, dinner. Closed Aug 🚇 Opéra

CHEZ PAUL €–€€

chezpaul.com

One of the last authentic Paris bistros serves staples such as snails and onion soup at very reasonable prices. Just like the menu, the decor hasn't been changed in decades, which makes it all the more fun.

🔲 Off map ✉ 13 rue de Charonne, 75011 ☎ 01 47 00 34 57 🕐 Daily lunch, dinner 🚇 Bastille, Ledru Rollin

LE COMPTOIR €€

hotel-paris-relais-saint-germain.com

At the vanguard of the movement, this gastro-bistro, under the expert eye of chef Yves Camdeborde, champions modern French cuisine. Reservations are not taken for lunch, but it's best to reserve ahead for dinner.

➕ H7 ✉ Hôtel Relais Saint-Germain, 9 carrefour de l'Odéon, 75006 ☎ 01 44 27 07 97 🕐 Daily lunch, dinner 🚇 Odéon

LA COUPOLE €€

lacoupole-paris.com

In business since 1927, this Montparnasse brasserie offers reasonably priced set menus plus all the standard dishes, but the elegant art deco setting and buzzy ambience are what make this place memorable.

➕ F9 ✉ 102 boulevard du Montparnasse, 75014 ☎ 01 43 20 14 20 🕐 Daily lunch, dinner 🚇 Vavin

Delectable oysters

DESI ROAD €€

desiroadrestaurant.com

One of the city's best Indian restaurants, with beautiful decor and attentive service, Desi Road serves a range of traditional curries.

➕ H6 ✉ 14 rue Dauphine, 75006 ☎ 01 43 26 44 91 🕐 Tue–Sun lunch, dinner 🚇 Pont Neuf, Odéon

EPICURE €€€

lebristolparis.com

Eric Frechon's superb restaurant offers the epitome of French gastronomic dining within the magnificent Bristol Hotel. Expect an inventive menu to titillate the taste buds. Attractive gardens are ideal for an alfresco dinner.

➕ D3 ✉ 112 rue du Faubourg Saint-Honoré, 75008 ☎ 01 53 43 43 00 🕐 Daily breakfast, lunch, dinner 🚇 Saint-Philippe du Roule

GORDON RAMSAY AU TRIANON €€€

gordonramsay.com

Round off a day of splendor in spectacular Versailles with a sumptuous dinner in Gordon Ramsay's much-praised dining room in the Trianon Palace Hotel, where the menu makes lavish use of luxurious ingredients such as lobster and foie gras.

➕ Off map ✉ 1 boulevard de la Reine, 78000, Versailles ☎ 01 30 84 50 18 🕐 Tue–Sat dinner 🚉 SNCF Versailles Rive Droite or RER Versailles Rive Gauche

NEW BISTROS

Paris may be the food capital of the world, with more than its share of top restaurants, but not everyone can afford the astronomical prices of the best eateries. Some 15 years ago a few famous chefs rebelled against this situation and opened "baby bistros," which offered fine meals in often nondescript surroundings for reasonable prices. The trend has now expanded and Paris is full of nouveaux bistros.

GUY SAVOY €€€

guysavoy.com

At this gastronomic temple, in a stunning new home at La Monnaie de Paris (Paris Mint building), chef Guy Savoy turns cooking into an art form. It is expensive to dine here, of course, but it is also exquisite; expect an unforgettable dining experience.

➕ H6 ✉ Monnaie de Paris, 11 quai de Conti, 75006 ☎ 01 43 80 40 61 🕐 Tue–Fri lunch, dinner, Sat dinner 🚇 Pont Neuf

LE JULES VERNE €€€

lejulesverne-paris.com

Alain Ducasse's wonderful restaurant can be found 125m (410ft) above the streets of Paris on level two of the Eiffel Tower. Since it opened in 2007, Le Jules Verne has been unequalled for its combination of superb food and fabulous panoramic day and nighttime views. Reservations are essential here.

➕ B6 ✉ 2nd level, Tour Eiffel, 75007 (private elevator) ☎ 01 45 55 61 44 🕐 Daily lunch, dinner 🚇 Bir-Hakeim

MIDI 12 €

midi12.com

This tiny, bright, modern café serves beautifully presented sweet and savory *crêpes* and *galettes* throughout the afternoon, which makes it an excellent pit stop for a quick yet filling lunch after a morning shopping on Boulevard Haussmann. It's a good option for vegans and vegetarians, and the soups and desserts also come highly recommended.

➕ G2 ✉ 12 rue la Fayette, 75009 ☎ 09 50 12 24 24 🕐 Mon–Fri noon–5.30pm, Sat 8.30–10am, noon–5.30pm 🚇 Chaussée d'Antin–La Fayette

---

LOCAL WINE

At the intersection of rue Saule and rue Saint-Vincent there is a small hillside of vines—a remnant of the former vineyards of the Butte Montmartre. During the wine harvest there is a very popular, colorful festival with plenty of tastings. For more information, visit fetedesvendanges demontmartre.com.

MONJUL €€

monjul.com

At Monjul, the talented Julien Agobert, one of an exciting new generation of daring and experimental chefs, produces exciting and inventive dishes that are works of art—and taste just as good, if not better, than they look. There's liberal use of pretty, edible flowers that give the dishes a certain picturesque quality.

➕ K5 ✉ 28 rue des Blancs Manteaux, 75004 ☎ 01 42 74 40 15 🕐 Tue–Sat lunch, dinner 🚇 Rambuteau

LES PAPILLES €–€€

lespapillesparis.fr

The authentic decor sets you up for a genuine bistro experience where you can choose from a daily set menu of French dishes made with market-fresh ingredients. There's also a wine and fine food store.

➕ H8 ✉ 30 rue Gay-Lussac, 75005 ☎ 01 43 25 20 79 🕐 Tue–Sat lunch, dinner 🚇 RER Luxembourg

LE PETIT SAINT-BENOÎT €

petit-st-benoit.com

This popular, inexpensive classic was once the haunt of writers; the decor has barely changed since the 1930s. The menu features a long list of French classics ranging from frogs' legs to boeuf bourguignon.

EAT

Taillevent is renowned for good food

🕂 G6　✉ 4 rue Saint-Benoît, 75006
☎ 01 42 60 27 92　⏰ Mon–Sat lunch,
dinner　🚇 Saint-Germain-des-Prés

LA PETITE ARDOISE €–€€

restaurantlapetiteardoise.fr

A popular restaurant in Fontainebleau, this serves classic French dishes from a variety of regions, as small or large servings.

🕂 Off map　✉ 16 rue Montebello, 77300
Fontainebleau　☎ 01 64 24 08 66　⏰ Tue–
Sat lunch, dinner　🚇 Fontainebleau–Avon

PINK MAMMA €€

bigmammagroup.com

A fun and authentically styled trattoria spread over four floors, each with a different decor style. The menu is filled with Italian staples, with a few fashionable extras such as burritos.

🕂 G1　✉ 20b rue de Douai, 75009
☎ 09 83 55 94 52　⏰ Daily lunch and
dinner (no reservations)　🚇 Pigalle

PRAMIL €–€€

pramil.fr

With a menu based on seasonal produce, Alain Pramil has built up

a loyal customer base. The presentation is refined and all at prices that make this one of Paris's best bistros in this price range.

🕂 L4　✉ 9 rue du Vertbois　☎ 01 42 77
03 60　⏰ Tue–Sat lunch, dinner, Sun
dinner　🚇 Arts et Métiers, Temple

LE PROGRÈS €–€€

This is the kind of café where you'd expect to see a character from the 2001 film *Amélie*, which was shot in the area. The staff provide expert service and the *plat du jour* is a big draw for the lunchtime crowds.

🕂 c2　✉ 7 rue des Trois-Frères, 75018
☎ 01 42 64 07 37　⏰ Daily 9am–2am
🚇 Abbesses

RESTAURANT FRENCHIE €€

frenchie-restaurant.com

This massively popular nouveau bistro is owned by Gregory Marchand, who worked with Jamie Oliver in London before returning to his native France. The menu is limited but the fusion dishes are superb. The only downside is that you'll need to reserve at least a month ahead to be sure of getting a table. Try Marchand's wine bar across the street if Frenchie is full.

🕂 J4　✉ 5–6 rue du Nil, 75002　☎ 01 40
39 96 19　⏰ Mon–Fri dinner, Thu–Fri lunch
(reservations obligatory)　🚇 Sentier

ROSE BAKERY €–€€

Organic food is served in this English bakery and tea shop, owned by a Franco-British couple. It is also a popular place for Sunday brunch.

🕂 c3　✉ 46 rue des Martyrs, 75009
☎ 01 42 82 12 80　⏰ Daily 9–6
(menu items 11–5.30)　🚇 Pigalle,
Notre-Dame-de-Lorette

SEB'ON €€

seb-on.com

One of the best in a bunch of modern bistros that have sprung up in the Montmartre area, Seb'on is a tiny place presided over by Sebastien Heloin. He serves a small and ever-changing daily menu of market-fresh dishes with suitably impressive results.

🗺 H1 ✉ 62 rue d'Orsel, 75018 ☎ 01 42 59 74 32 🕐 Sun lunch, Wed–Sat dinner 🚇 Abbesses

SEPTIME €€–€€€

septime-charonne.fr

One of a new generation of fine-dining restaurants in Paris, Septime has quickly built legions of loyal patrons, though you'll have to surrender yourself to chef Bertrand Grebaut's fixed menu for dinner (you'll be asked about any food allergies before you are served). Lunch offers good value.

🗺 Off map ✉ 80 rue de Charonne, 75011 ☎ 01 43 67 38 29 🕐 Mon dinner, Tue–Fri lunch, dinner 🚇 Charonne

TAILLEVENT €€€

taillevent.com

The cooking at this elegant restaurant features classical foundations with subtle modern leanings. Opened some 70 years ago, it steadily gained in popularity and is worthy of its fine reputation.

🗺 C2 ✉ 15 rue Lamennais, 75008 ☎ 01 44 95 15 01 🕐 Mon–Fri lunch, dinner. Closed late Jul to mid-Aug 🚇 George V, Charles de Gaulle–Étoile

TANNAT €€

tannat.fr

Classically trained Olivier Le Corre presides over the kitchen of one of the city's popular nouveau bistros.

The short menu allows his team to concentrate on ingredients in their seasonal prime and the bio vegetables are all from one producer to ensure freshness and quality.

🗺 M3 ✉ 119 avenue Parmentier, 75011 ☎ 09 53 86 38 61 🕐 Mon–Fri lunch and dinner, Sun–Mon lunch 🚇 Place Monge

LA TOUR D'ARGENT €€€

latourdargent.com

Come to this historic fine-dining restaurant in the Latin Quarter for its spectacular view, its extensive wine cellar and the exceptionally tasty duck. It is quite superb.

🗺 K7 ✉ 15–17 quai de la Tournelle, 75005 (facing Île Saint-Louis) ☎ 01 43 54 23 31 🕐 Tue–Sat lunch, dinner. Closed Aug 🚇 Maubert–Mutualité

ZE KITCHEN GALERIE €€

zekitchengalerie.fr

The inventive cuisine at this chic restaurant has been rewarded with a Michelin star. Chef William Ledeuil combines the tastes and textures of southeast Asia with French techniques to produce creative dishes using French-grown fresh produce.

🗺 H6 ✉ 4 rue des Grands-Augustins, 75006 ☎ 01 44 32 00 32 🕐 Mon–Fri lunch, dinner 🚇 Odéon

EAT

PICNIC LUNCHES

If your taste is for a *déjeuner sur l'herbe* in Fontainebleau, the rue Grande grocery stores are perfect for picnic supplies. In Versailles, the Marché Notre-Dame is an excellent covered market (closed on Mondays) for stocking up on lunch items. When in Chantilly, allow yourself to be tempted by the bakeries, with their delicious cakes and pastries filled with lashings of the eponymous cream.

Sleep

Paris has a great range of places to stay, with options to suit all tastes and budgets. In this section, establishments are listed alphabetically.

SLEEP

Introduction

The city's hotels have seen an overhaul in recent years. Boutique hotels have sprung up all over Paris, especially in the Marais. Hotels around the Louvre, Champs-Élysées and Opéra tend to be more expensive, while those in the Latin Quarter are often smaller and more affordable.

Finding a Good Deal
Some of the luxury hotels are out of another era. Their stated prices are high but discounts can be found online or through some travel agents. Paris is one of the rare European capitals where you can find a pleasant, affordable place to stay in a central part of the city. The Paris Tourist Office (▷ 167) has information. You can reserve rooms if you visit in person.

Helpful Tips
Prices often drop in July and August and rise in May, June, September and October, for the trade fairs. Check whether the price includes breakfast. If you are bringing or renting a car, ask whether parking is available and the cost.

Outer Limits
Chain hotels on the outskirts can be less expensive, but they lack character. You'll also have to spend more time taking the Métro.

APARTMENT LIVING

● To rent an apartment in Paris, options include the UK-based Apartment Service (from the UK, tel 020 8944 1444; from the US tel 011 44 20 8944 1444 or write to 709 Plaza Drive Suite 2, #299 Chicago, IL 46304, apartmentservice.com) and Home Rental Service at 120 avenue des Champs-Élysées, 75008 (tel 01 42 25 65 40, homerental.fr).

● For bed-and-breakfast, try France Lodge at 12 rue Truffaut, 75017 (tel 01 56 33 85 85, francelodge.fr) and Bed & Breakfast France, rue des Tulipes, 85100 Les Sables D'Olonne (tel 09 60 09 86 49, bedbreak.com).

From top: Yooma; the lobby of Le Meurice; let someone else take the strain with your luggage; a junior suite at Le Meurice

SLEEP

Directory

AROUND THE TOUR EIFFEL
Budget
Hôtel de l'Avre
Yooma Paris Tour Eiffel

LATIN QUARTER, ST-GERMAIN AND ISLANDS
Budget
The Five Hotel
Hôtel du Collège de France
Hôtel des Nations Saint-Germain
Mid-Range
Hôtel d'Angleterre
Hôtel Design de la Sorbonne
Hôtel Duc de Saint-Simon
Hôtel des Marronniers
Hôtel La Perle
Hôtel Sainte-Beuve
Hôtel de l'Université
Les Rives de Notre-Dame
Luxury
L'Hôtel
Hôtel de l'Abbaye
Hôtel du Jeu de Paume

MARAIS AND BASTILLE
Budget
Hôtel de la Place des Vosges
Mid-Range
Hôtel Caron de Beaumarchais
Hôtel Jules et Jim
Luxury
1K
Pavillon de la Reine

LOUVRE AND CHAMPS-ÉLYSÉES
Mid-Range
Hôtel Crayon
Hôtel Molière
Luxury
Hôtel San Régis
Le Meurice

MONTMARTRE
Mid-Range
Hôtel 29 Lepic
Hotel Terrass

Sleeping A–Z

PRICES
Prices are approximate and based on a double room for one night.

€€€	€251–€800
€€	€151–€250
€	€50–€150

1K €€–€€€
1K-paris.com
Sharp modern design, variable lighting effects and great attention to detail characterize this splendid boutique hotel. There are 43 rooms and 9 suites (some rooms have an interior courtyard view), a highly popular bar, a relaxing covered terrace as well as an in-house restaurant.
➕ M4 ✉ 13 boulevard du Temple, 75003 ☎ 01 42 71 20 00 🚇 Filles du Calvaire

THE FIVE HOTEL €
thefivehotel.com
Quality touches point to a high standard at this budget boutique hotel. There's no doubt that the rooms here are very small but what they lack in space, they make up for in style, with their clean lines and bold blocks of color.
➕ J9 ✉ 3 rue Flatters, 75005 ☎ 01 43 31 74 21 🚇 Gobelins

L'HÔTEL €€€

l-hotel.com

A Parisian legend, L'Hôtel is exuberantly elegant and intimate. Oscar Wilde stayed here, and celebrities can often be found in the discreet bar. There are 20 individually styled rooms, some superbly appointed, as well as a hammam pool where guests can relax, and a restaurant.

✚ G6 ✉ 13 rue des Beaux-Arts, 75006 ☎ 01 44 41 99 00 🚇 Saint-Germain-des-Prés

HÔTEL 29 LEPIC €–€€

29lepic.fr

This three-star hotel is near the Sacré-Cœur. Its simple but bright bedrooms have been carefully furnished. There's free WiFi throughout and generous breakfast hours of 7am until 11am, perfect after late nights or for jetlag.

✚ b2 ✉ 29 rue Lepic, 75018 ☎ 01 56 55 50 04 🚇 Blanche, Abbesses

HÔTEL DE L'ABBAYE €€€

hotelabbayeparis.com

This quaint and historic hotel was once a convent but now has a country house atmosphere.

BUDGET HOTELS

Gone are the heady days when Paris was peppered with atmospheric basic hotels with their inimitable signs "eau à tous les étages" (water on every floor). Now there are usually bath or shower rooms with every bedroom, resulting in higher prices and smaller rooms. So don't expect much space in budget hotel rooms, and be aware that breakfast may not be included. Receptionists usually speak a second language in hotels with two or more stars.

The lounge and most of the 40 rooms overlook a patio, and there's a cozy bar on site.

✚ G7 ✉ 10 rue Cassette, 75006 ☎ 01 45 44 38 11 🚇 Saint-Sulpice

HÔTEL D'ANGLETERRE €€

hotel-dangleterre.com

This former 18th-century British embassy has a garden patio and individually appointed, spacious rooms with an elegant period feel. Ernest Hemingway lived in room 14 in 1921. There is a bar and a relaxing piano lounge.

✚ G6 ✉ 44 rue Jacob, 75006 ☎ 01 42 60 34 72 🚇 Saint-Germain-des-Prés

HÔTEL DE L'AVRE €

hoteldelavre.com

This impeccably kept two-star hotel is justifiably popular with guests. The 25 individually decorated rooms vary in size and some look out over the rear courtyard. Breakfast is served in the pretty garden in spring and summer.

✚ B8 ✉ 21 rue de l'Avre, 75015 ☎ 01 45 75 31 03 🚇 La Motte-Picquet–Grenelle

HÔTEL CARON DE BEAUMARCHAIS €€

carondebeaumarchais.com

Set in a period townhouse styled to evoke the Age of Enlightenment, the 19 rooms are compact but beautifully furnished in period style, with sumptuous fabrics and elegant wallpapers used throughout. There's still modern touches like WiFi, air conditioning and an elevator, but lovers of clean mini-malism should book elsewhere.

✚ K6 ✉ 12 rue Vieille-du-Temple, 75004 ☎ 01 42 72 34 12 🚇 Saint-Paul

HÔTEL DU COLLÈGE DE FRANCE €–€€

hotel-collegedefrance.com

This inexpensive family-owned hotel is set behind a Haussmann-designed facade. There are 29 well-presented simple but modern rooms that vary in size. All are en suite; some have small balconies overlooking the street.

🟦 J7 ✉ 7 rue Thénard, 75005 ☎ 01 43 26 78 36 🚇 Maubert–Mutualité

HÔTEL CRAYON €€

hotelcrayon.com

The creation of artist Julie Gauthron, this boutique hotel has individually styled rooms filled with items chosen by Julie herself. It is a contemporary space and some of the rooms are in-your-face bright; check the website before booking.

🟦 H4 ✉ 25 rue du Bouloi, 75001 ☎ 01 42 36 54 19 🚇 Louvre–Rivoli, Les Halles

HÔTEL DESIGN DE LA SORBONNE €–€€

hotelsorbonne.com

This hotel has contemporary living down to a fine art. Each floor has photos, engravings and literary quotes that complement the British-style decor. The 38 bedrooms have iMac computers, among the lavish facilities.

🟦 H8 ✉ 6 rue Victor-Cousin, 75005 ☎ 01 43 54 58 08 🚇 Cluny–La Sorbonne

HÔTEL DUC DE SAINT-SIMON €€

hotelducdesaintsimon.com

This elegant 18th-century town-house has been transformed into a small hotel with delightful period styling. It is pricey (at the top end of mid-range) but the antiques and setting, just off boulevard Saint-Germain, justify this. There are 34 comfortable rooms.

🟦 F6 ✉ 14 rue Saint-Simon, 75007 ☎ 01 44 39 20 20 🚇 Rue du Bac

HÔTEL DU JEU DE PAUME €€€

jeudepaumehotel.com

This small, delightful hotel is carved out of a 17th-century royal tennis court. The interior is a surprise considering the age of the buildings, with many contemporary touches. There are 30 tasteful rooms and two large apartments for longer rentals.

🟦 K7 ✉ 54 rue Saint-Louis-en-l'Île, 75004 ☎ 01 43 26 14 18 🚇 Pont Marie

HÔTEL JULES ET JIM €€–€€€

hoteljulesetjim.com

Three town houses come together in a contemporary ensemble that's named after a François Truffaut film. The public spaces double as a photographic gallery. Rooms come in different styles and sizes, but they are all well furnished. The bar is a popular meeting place for events, and breakfast hours are long. There's an outside courtyard to enjoy in summer.

🟦 K4 ✉ 11 rue des Gravilliers, 75003 ☎ 01 44 54 13 13 🚇 Arts et Métiers

HÔTEL DES MARRONNIERS €€

hoteldesmarronniers.com

The oak-beamed rooms and vaulted cellars here have been converted into relaxing lounges. There are 37 well-appointed and comfortable guest rooms; request one with a view of the garden. There's also a lovely *salon du thé*.

🟦 G6 ✉ 21 rue Jacob, 75006 ☎ 01 43 25 30 60 🚇 Saint-Germain-des-Prés

HÔTEL MOLIÈRE €€

hotel-moliere.fr

A small boutique hotel, the Molière has calm zen-like interiors. There are 32 rooms, one with a good-sized balcony. The bathrooms are tiny but contemporary. There's a sauna/wellness/fitness center on site, but no restaurant.

➕ G4 ✉ 21 rue Molière, 75001 ☎ 01 42 96 22 01 Ⓜ Pyramides, Palais-Royal

HÔTEL DES NATIONS SAINT-GERMAIN €–€€

paris-hotel-des-nations-st-germain.com

A modern hotel with contemporary decoration and delightful style touches, this small hotel has compact but well-equipped rooms. There is also an honesty bar here, and free WiFi is available in all the rooms.

➕ K8 ✉ 54 rue Monge, 75005 ☎ 01 43 26 45 24 Ⓜ Cardinal Lemoine

HÔTEL LA PERLE €€

hotel-paris-laperle.com

This renovated 17th-century building on a quiet street has 38 rooms. It lies at the upper end of the mid-range price bracket, but the attention to detail, room decor and spacious communal areas are well worth the price. The large veranda is a charming setting for

---

LE CRILLON

Whether you stay at the Ritz, the Crillon, the Meurice, the Bristol or the Georges V, they all have interesting tales to tell, but that of the Crillon is perhaps the most momentous. This mansion managed to survive the Revolution despite having the guillotine on its doorstep. Mary Pickford and Douglas Fairbanks spent their honeymoon here.

---

evening drinks and there's also a fitness room.

➕ G7 ✉ 14 rue des Canettes, 75006 ☎ 01 43 29 10 10 Ⓜ Mabillon

HÔTEL DE LA PLACE DES VOSGES €

hotelplacedesvosges.com

This 17th-century townhouse in the Marais offers minimalist styling, mixing period furniture and architectural details with stark white walls.

➕ M6 ✉ 12 rue de Birague, 75004 ☎ 01 42 72 60 46 Ⓜ Bastille, Saint-Paul

HÔTEL SAINTE-BEUVE €€–€€€

hotelsaintebeuve.com

Between Montparnasse and the Luxembourg gardens, this club-like exclusive hotel features a stylish blend of period antiques and modern furnishings. Standard rooms are small, but there are connecting rooms to cater for families and groups.

➕ G8 ✉ 9 rue Sainte-Beuve, 75006 ☎ 01 45 48 20 07 Ⓜ Notre-Dame-des-Champs

HÔTEL SAN RÉGIS €€€

hotel-sanregis.fr

Popular with showbiz folk, this hotel has 31 rooms and 11 suites. Interior designer Pierre-Yves Rochon mixes antique pieces with ornate chintz to re-create classic French Empire style. It's certainly exclusive, with prices to match.

➕ D4 ✉ 12 rue Jean-Goujon, 75008 ☎ 01 44 95 16 16 Ⓜ Franklin D. Roosevelt, Champs-Élysées–Clémenceau

HÔTEL TERRASS €–€€

terrass-hotel.com

It's been open since 1911, but the interior of this boutique

Mid-priced establishments are popular with business visitors, so it is virtually impossible to find rooms during the trade-fair seasons (May to early June and mid-September to October). In summer, many offer discounts as their occupancy shrinks. All rooms are equipped with TV, phone, private bath or shower rooms and minibar, and most supply a hairdryer. Air-conditioning is not standard, but elevators are common.

Montmartre hotel is cool and contemporary. Rooms have designer touches and bold splashes of color. There's a small spa and a lovely terrace restaurant with views across Paris.

➕ B1 ✉ 12–15 rue Joseph de Maistre, 75018 ☎ 01 46 06 72 85 🚇 Blanche

HÔTEL DE L'UNIVERSITÉ €€

universitehotel.com

This Left Bank hotel *par excellence* has 27 rooms, some complete with (nonworking) fireplaces, antique furnishings and exposed beams. The pastel decor in the rooms and communal areas offers a calming refuge from city hustle and bustle after a busy day of sightseeing.

➕ G6 ✉ 22 rue de l'Université, 75007 ☎ 01 42 61 09 39 🚇 Rue du Bac

LE MEURICE €€€

dorchestercollection.com

Situated just across the street from the Louvre, this historic 18th-century hotel has been thoroughly modernized, but the luxurious furnishings in the 160 rooms have more than a touch of Louis XVI style and elegance about them. French master chef Alain Ducasse stamps his inimitable mark on the dining experience here.

➕ F5 ✉ 228 rue de Rivoli, 75001 ☎ 01 44 58 10 10 🚇 Concorde, Tuileries

PAVILLON DE LA REINE €€€

pavillon-de-la-reine.com

Period decoration and lavish furnishings in this 17th-century building are enhanced by the peaceful and leafy garden. There are 56 rooms and suites. The hotel has a small spa but it does not have a restaurant.

➕ M6 ✉ 28 place des Vosges, 75003 ☎ 01 40 29 19 19 🚇 Bastille, Chemin Vert

LES RIVES DE NOTRE-DAME €€–€€€

rivesdenotredame.com

Overlooking the banks of the Seine, this hotel has beamed ceilings, marble tiling, tapestries and fine wrought-iron furniture. It's a small property of only 10 rooms, so you are guaranteed an intimate atmosphere and a warm welcome. There are wonderful views of the river and also to Notre-Dame from some of the rooms.

➕ J7 ✉ 15 quai Saint-Michel, 75005 ☎ 01 43 54 81 16 🚇 Saint-Michel

YOOMA PARIS TOUR EIFFEL €

yooma-hotels.com

An example of contemporary design by Ora Ïto and Daniel Buren on the banks of the Seine, this is a 21st-century eco-hotel of 106 rooms with capacities for two to six people; perfect for families or groups. A roof garden grows vegetables for the restaurant.

➕ A7 ✉ 51 quai de Grenelle, 75015 ☎ 01 44 09 00 13 🚇 Bir Hakeim

SLEEP

Need to Know

This section takes you through all the practical aspects of your trip to make it run more smoothly and to give you confidence before you go and while you are there.

NEED TO KNOW

Planning Ahead

WHEN TO GO

Spring is popular, when the chestnut trees are in blossom. The city reaches peak tourist capacity in hot, sunny July. However, with the Parisian exodus to the countryside in August the city is emptier than usual. Fall is busy with trade fairs and rooms can be scarce and expensive.

TEMPERATURE

JAN	FEB	MAR	APR	MAY	JUN	JUL	AUG	SEP	OCT	NOV	DEC
6°C	7°C	12°C	16°C	20°C	23°C	25°C	26°C	21°C	16°C	10°C	7°C
43°F	45°F	54°F	61°F	68°F	73°F	77°F	79°F	70°F	61°F	50°F	45°F

Spring (April, May) takes time to get going. Things don't usually warm up until mid-May.
Summer (June to August) can be glorious. Days are longest in June, with the most sunshine and a pleasant temperature. It is usually hot and sunny in July, and often hot, humid and stormy in August.
Fall (September to November) has crisp days and usually clear skies.
Winter (December to March) is rarely below freezing but it rains frequently, sometimes with hail, in January and March.

WHAT'S ON

January/February *Chinese New Year:* In Chinatown, 13th *arrondissement.*
April/May *International Paris Fair:* Consumer heaven at Porte de Versailles, foire deparis.fr.
Paris marathon: Starts from the Champs-Élysées, schneiderelectric parismarathon.com.
May *Labor Day* (1 May): Parades and symbolic lily-of-the-valley bouquets.
La Nuit des Musées: On the third Saturday evening museums fling their doors open with music, drama and readings.
June *Paris Jazz Festival* (mid-Jun to Jul): Weekends at Parc Floral de Paris (parisjazzfestival.fr).
Fête de la Musique (21 Jun): Music on the streets.
La Marche des Fiertés LGBTQ+ de Paris (Gay Pride) (Sat in late Jun): Popular procession, plus partying in the Marais.
July *Bastille Day* (14 Jul): The most important French festival celebrates the 1789 storming of the Bastille. Fireworks and street dances on the evening of the 13th and a parade on the 14th on the Champs-Élysées.
July–August *Festival Paris l'Été:* Outdoor performances, quartierdete.com.
Paris Plages: Beaches along the quays of the Seine.
September *Festival d'Automne à Paris* (mid-Sep to Dec): Music, theater and dance all over the city, festival-automne.com.
October *Foire Internationale d'Art Contemporain:* Paris's biggest modern art fair, fiac.com.
Nuit Blanche: For one night various cultural venues open all night, free.
November *Beaujolais Nouveau* (third Thu in Nov): Drinking in all the city's bars.
December *Paris International Boat Show* salonnautiqueparis.com.

PARIS ONLINE
visitparisregion.com
The website of the Paris Île de France regional tourist authority has a huge quantity and variety of information on Paris and the surrounding region, including entertainment and events, shopping, sport and leisure, children's Paris, accommodations and public transportation. It now has a new site dedicated to English-language speakers.

parisinfo.com
The Paris Tourist Office online has listings and practical information, sightseeing and links to other useful sites covering every aspect of leisure in the city. It also provides an online hotel booking service.

parisbymouth.com
Information for foodies, or someone looking for the latest hot bistro, rising star chef or up-coming food festivals in the city.

parisvoice.com
Intended for English-speaking Parisians, this site gives an insider's view of the city, with features, events information, restaurant reviews, classified ads, a Q&A column (dealing with some very serious issues) and more.

paris.fr
The official site of Paris's mayor and city council has information on museums, theaters, parks and sport, as well as a virtual tour of the Hôtel de Ville. There is also a wealth of civic news aimed at Paris residents.

france.fr
The official website for the French tourist authority has information for the whole of France, but Paris features heavily. Find the latest exhibition and concert information, plus practical information about your stay in France.

parisupdate.com
What's happening, updated weekly: art shows, films, restaurants, concerts.

TRAVEL SITES
parisdigest.com
Independent guide showing you around the city with mainstream practical information. A good range of hotel, restaurant and shopping guides.

fodors.com
A complete travel-planning site. You can research prices; book air tickets, cars and rooms; ask questions (and get answers) from fellow travelers; and find links to other sites.

PARIS WIFI
There is free access to WiFi in almost 300 parks, libraries and public buildings in Paris. Hot spots are shown with distinctive oval signs. You'll need to link to PARIS_WI-FI_ page, create a password, fill in a form and agree to terms. Each free session lasts up to two hours.

Getting There

GETTING YOUR BEARINGS

Think of Paris as a snail, with its shell curling around the 1st *arrondissement* (district) right in the middle. The numbers of the other *arrondissements* follow clockwise, ending with the 20th on the eastern side of the city. *C'est logique, non*?

AIRPORTS

Most international flights arrive at Roissy Charles de Gaulle Airport, with some international and French domestic flights arriving at Orly Airport. Paris has good rail connections, including the Eurostar train direct from London.

Roissy Charles de Gaulle Airport
Bus 50 mins, €12/€18
Train 35 mins, €10.30

Orly Airport
Bus 30 mins, €10

60km (40 miles)

FROM ROISSY CHARLES DE GAULLE

Roissy (tel 3950, outside France 331 70 36 39 50, adp.fr) is 23km (14 miles) northeast of central Paris and has three terminals. Air France currently operates out of Terminal 2. There are three ways to get to the city.

By bus: Le Bus Direct (lebusdirect.com) operates a bus service (Line 4) between the airport and Montparnasse and Gare de Lyon, every 30 minutes 5.45am–10.45pm (€18), and to the Arc de Triomphe (Étoile) and Porte Maillot (Line 2) every 20–30 minutes, 5am–11pm (€18). Buy tickets from the driver (€1 extra) or at the Air France offices in the terminal, or take the 50-minute trip on Roissybus that runs every 15 or 20 minutes from Terminals 1, 2 and 3 to Opéra, 6am–12.30am (€12).

By train: The RER (Réseau Express Régional) Line B takes around 35 minutes to reach central Paris (€10.30). Trains leave every 10–15 minutes.

By taxi: There are fixed-rate fares between the airport and the downtown core. Fares are €50 to destinations on the left bank of the River Seine and €55 to destinations on the right bank. There's a €4 reservation fee (€7 if booked in advance).

FROM ORLY

Orly (tel 3950, outside France 331 70 36 39 50, adp.fr), the smaller of Paris's two main international airports, is 14km (8.5 miles) from central Paris, with no direct train to the city.

By bus: Le Bus Direct provides shuttle buses to Les Invalides, Étoile and Gare Montparnasse every 20–30 minutes, 4.40am–9.45pm (about 30 minutes; €10 single/€22 return).

By train: The Orlyval train, which operates daily 6am–11.35pm, will take you to Antony, where you can change for Line B of the RER rail system (€9.30). From here, it's around 25 minutes to central Paris.

By taxi: A taxi costs €30 to destinations on the left bank of the River Seine and €35 to destinations on the right bank and takes 15–30 minutes.

EUROSTAR

The Eurostar (tel 01 70 70 60 88 in France, 03432 186 186 in the UK, eurostar.com) takes you from London to the Gare du Nord in the heart of Paris in about 2 hours 15 minutes. From here, there are good Métro and RER connections, or you can take a taxi.

THALYS

Thalys (tel 0825 84 25 97, thalys.com) offers daily high-speed train services linking Paris to large cities such as Brussels, Antwerp, Amsterdam, Cologne and Dortmund.

BUDGET OPTIONS

Within Europe, low-cost airlines such as easyJet (easyjet.com) and Ryanair (ryanair.com) offer some attractive and competitive prices that can sometimes beat the cost of traveling by train. But the tickets are not always bargains; they are priced according to availability and demand. It is usually best to book as far in advance as possible. Keep in mind that Ryanair flies in and out of Beauvais airport, 70km (43 miles) from Paris, so the low cost of a ticket may not be worth the time lost in traveling to and from the airport. EasyJet uses Roissy Charles de Gaulle Airport for flights from the UK.

VISAS AND TRAVEL INSURANCE

Visas are not required for EU, US or Canadian nationals, but you will need a valid passport. (Check the latest requirements before you travel.) EU citizens receive reduced-cost medical treatment with the European Health Insurance Card (EHIC). Full insurance is still strongly advised and is essential for all other travelers.

BREXIT

UK visitors should check the very latest entry requirements as a result of the country's decision to leave the EU. Check if a visa is required along with a valid passport and if reduced-cost medical treatment with the European Health Insurance Card (EHIC) is still available. Visit gov.uk/visit-europe-brexit.

Getting Around

VISITORS WITH DISABILITIES

Paris has a mixed record on access and amenities. On the Métro, only the Meteor line (No. 14) has easy access for people with disabilities. Since 2009, all bus lines in the city are wheelchair accessible and 80 percent of the bus stops have been specially adapted. Vianavigo (☎ 09 70 81 83 85, vianavigo.com) is a service with information and news about public transportation for visitors with a disability. RATP's Les Compagnons du Voyage (☎ 01 58 76 08 33, compagnons.com) provides companions for visitors with disabilities (if not in an electric wheelchair), but for a fee. Two taxi companies, G7 (☎ 01 41 27 66 99, taxisg7.com) and Taxis PMR (☎ 06 14 67 75 02, taxipmr.onlc.fr), will take wheelchairs. The website of the Paris Tourist Office (parisinfo.com) has information for visitors with disabilities, including a list of the city's accessible sights. The downloadable *Accessible Paris* guide has more information about getting around, and can be accessed on the Paris Tourist Office website.

MÉTRO

The best way to travel around Paris is by Métro or RER, two separate but linked systems (ratp.fr). The RER is the suburban line, which passes through the heart of the city. The Métro is the underground system, with 14 main lines and 303 stations. Both are inexpensive and efficient, and free maps of all the routes are available at station ticket windows. Any place is within easy walking distance of a Métro or RER station. Both systems function in the same way and the tickets are interchangeable within the city. It is cheaper to buy a *carnet* of 10 tickets than to buy each ticket separately.

● Métro lines are always identified by their destination and a number; connections are shown in *correspondances* panels displayed on the platform.

● The first Métros run at 5.30am, and the last around 1.15am (2.15am Fri and Sat).

● Keep your ticket until you exit—it has to be reinserted on the RER, and ticket inspectors prowl the Métro.

TICKETS AND PASSES

● Tickets and passes function for Métro, buses, trams and RER.

● One ticket (€1.90) gives access to zones 1 and 2 of the Métro network, the RER within Paris, trams and Parisian and suburban buses. A *carnet* of 10 tickets is €14.90.

● Single tickets (known as Ticket t+) are only valid for a single journey without changing between bus, Métro, tram and RER.

● Prices of passes and suburban RER tickets depend on how many travel zones you intend to pass through.

● Mobilis is a one-day pass, valid on the Métro, buses and RER.

● A Paris Visite card gives unlimited travel for one, two, three or five days plus discounts at certain monuments, but you need to do a lot of traveling to make it pay.

● *Navigo Découverte* travel cards for visitors are obtainable from stations and valid for a week *(Forfait Navigo Semaine)*, starting Monday and ending the following Sunday, or month *(Forfait*

Navigo Mois). Both are valid on routes from
the airports to downtown. You'll need to
provide a passport photo.

BATOBUS
Traveling by Batobus (river shuttle boat) is fun
(late-Apr to early Sep daily 10–9.30, every
25 minutes; late-Mar to late-Apr and early Sep
to early Nov, daily 10–7, every 20 minutes;
early-Nov to late-Mar Mon–Thu 10–5, every
40 minutes, Fri–Sun 10–7, every 40 minutes).
It stops at the Eiffel Tower, Musée d'Orsay,
Saint-Germain-des-Prés, Notre-Dame, Jardin
des Plantes, Hôtel de Ville, Louvre, Champs-
Élysées and Beaugrenelle. Join at any point.
An all-day ticket is €17, a two-day ticket costs
€19 (tel 08 25 05 01 01, batobus.com).

BICYCLES
Pick up bicycles and electric cycles from the
self-service stops across Paris, via the Vélib' hire
scheme (tel 01 76 49 12 34, velib-metropole.
fr). One-day (€5) or seven-day (€15) tickets
are available. The first 30 minutes' on non-
electric bikes is free. There is a small charge
per 30 minutes for all other journeys.

TAXIS
Taxis can be hailed in the street if the roof sign
is illuminated or at taxi ranks outside most
main attractions. There are three tariffs in
central Paris: A applies Mon–Sat 10am–5pm;
B applies Mon–Sat 5pm–10am, Sun 7am–
midnight and 24 hours on public holidays
Mon–Sat; C applies Sun midnight–7am.
There are extra charges for the fourth and fifth
passengers. Tip drivers 10 percent.
● The initial fee for hiring a taxi is €4 if booked
immediately, €7 if prebooked, or there's a
€2.60 pick up fee and the minimum fare is €7.
Tariff A is €1.07 per km, B €1.35 and C €1.60.
If luggage is more than 5kg (11 lbs), there is
an excess of €1.
● Taxi ranks that have telephones can be called
on 01 45 30 30 30. Select your *arrondissement*
with the help of the voice server, who will then
connect you to the closest rank.

STUDENT VISITORS
● An International Student
Identity Card can reduce
cinema charges, entrance
fees to museums and air
and rail travel.
● MIJE (Maison
Internationale de la
Jeunesse et des Étudiants)
✉ 6 rue Fourcy, 75004
☎ 01 42 74 23 45,
mije.com
Ⓜ Saint-Paul
🕐 Daily 7am–1am.
Three hostels for young
people in the heart of Paris.
● CIDJ (Centre
d'Information et de
Documentation Jeunesse)
✉ 101 quai Branly, 75015
☎ 01 44 49 12 00,
cidj.com
Ⓜ Bir-Hakeim
🕐 Tue–Fri 1–6, Sat 1–5.
Youth information office for
jobs, courses, sport.

TOURIST OFFICE
● Office du Tourisme de
Paris
✉ Hôtel de Ville, 29 rue du
Rivoli, 75004
☎ parisinfo.com
🕐 May–Oct daily 9–7;
Nov–Apr daily 10–7
Ⓜ Hotel de Ville
❓ There are English-
speaking staff in the tourist
office

Essential Facts

MONEY

The euro is the official currency of France. There are bank notes in denominations of €5, €10, €20, €50, €100 and €200 and coins in denominations of 1, 2, 5, 10, 20 and 50 cents and €1 and €2.

TIPPING

In every restaurant, by law, a 15 percent service charge and all relevant taxes are already in the prices on the menu. If the service was especially pleasant, or if you feel odd about leaving nothing, then you can leave another couple of euros or 5 percent. In taxis, it is customary to give the driver a 10 percent tip, but only if you are happy with the service.

CREDIT CARDS

● Credit cards are widely accepted.
● VISA cards are the most widely accepted and can be used in cash dispensers. Make sure you know your international PIN. MasterCard and Diners Club are also widely accepted.
● American Express is less common, so Amex cardholders requiring cash should look out for cash dispensers at post offices or check the information on the website americanexpress. com for other locations.

ETIQUETTE

● Shake hands on introduction and on leaving; once you know people well replace this with a peck on both cheeks.
● Always use *vous* unless the other person breaks into *tu*.
● It is polite to add *Monsieur, Madame* or *Mademoiselle* when addressing strangers.
● Always say *bonjour* and *au revoir* in shops.
● When calling waiters, use *Monsieur* or *Madame* (not *garçon*).
● Dress carefully. More emphasis is put on appearance in France than in other countries. Smart-casual dress is the norm.

FOREIGN EXCHANGE

● Only banks with Change signs will change foreign currency/traveler's checks; a passport is necessary for identification. Bureaux de change are open longer hours but rates can be poorer. Fees for cashing euro traveler's checks can be high.
● Airport and station exchange desks are open daily 6 or 6.30am to 10 or 10.30pm.

MEDICINES AND MEDICAL TREATMENT

● Minor ailments can often be treated at pharmacies.
● Public hospitals have a 24-hour emergency service *(urgences)* and specialist doctors. Payment is made on the spot, but if you are hospitalized see the *assistante sociale* to arrange payment through your insurance.
● House calls are made by SOS Médecins, tel 36 24 or 01 47 07 77 77, sosmedecins.fr.

• For dental problems, contact SOS Dentaire, tel 01 43 37 51 00, sos-dentaire.com.
• 24-hour pharmacy: Pharmacie de Champs-Élysées, 84 avenue des Champs-Élysées, 75008, tel 01 45 62 02 41.
• Publicis drugstore (133 avenue des Champs-Élysées, tel 01 44 43 79 00) is a pharmacy, café, newsagent and tobacconist, open until 2am. Its night pharmacy is open 2am–8am.
• Pharmacies display a green cross outside.

NATIONAL HOLIDAYS
• 1 January, Easter Monday, 1 May, 8 May, Ascension (a Thursday in May), Whit Monday (late May or early June), 14 July, 15 August, 1 November, 11 November, 25 December.
• Sunday services for public transportation operate; many local shops, restaurants and some large stores remain open on national holidays.

POST OFFICES
Stamps can be bought at *tabacs*; post mail in any yellow mailbox. All post offices offer express courier post (Chronopost).

PUBLIC TOILETS
• Public toilets are free and are generally well maintained, although they are not plentiful.
• The Point WCs, on the Champs-Élysées, at the Carrousel du Louvre, Metro Cluny–La Sorbonne, and on boulevard Haussmann, are "super loos," for €2.
• Malls and department stores have good public facilities and every café has a toilet, but order a drink too.

EMERGENCY NUMBERS
• Crisis-line in English: SOS Help ☎ 01 46 21 46 46, soshelpline.org
🕐 3pm–11pm
• Police ☎ 17
• Any emergency ☎ 112
• Ambulance (SAMU) ☎ 15
• Fire (*sapeurs pompiers*) ☎ 18
• Anti-poison ☎ 01 40 05 48 48
• Police lost-property office ✉ 36 rue des Morillons, 75015 ☎ 08 21 00 25 25

ELECTRICITY
• Voltage is 220V; French sockets take plugs with two round pins.

EMBASSIES/CONSULATES

US Embassy	✉ 2 avenue Gabriel, 75008 ☎ 01 43 12 22 22
US Consulate	✉ 4 avenue Gabriel, 75008 ☎ 01 43 12 22 22
Canadian Embassy	✉ 130 rue du Faubourg Saint-Honoré, 75008 ☎ 01 44 43 29 00
British Embassy	✉ 35 rue du Faubourg Saint-Honoré, 75008 ☎ 01 44 51 31 00
British Consulate	✉ 16 rue d'Anjou, 75008 ☎ 01 44 51 31 00
Australian Embassy	✉ 4 rue Jean-Rey, 75015 ☎ 01 40 59 33 00
New Zealand Embassy	✉ 103 rue de Grenelle, 75007 ☎ 01 45 01 43 43
Portuguese Embassy	✉ 1 rue de Noisiel, 75116 ☎ 01 47 27 35 29
Spanish Embassy	✉ 22 avenue Marceau, 75008 ☎ 01 44 43 18 00

● Banks: Mon–Fri 9–12.30, 2–5. Closed on public holidays and often the preceding afternoon.

● Post offices: Mon–Fri 8–7, Sat 8–12. The main post office (✉ 52 rue du Louvre, 75001) is open every day.

● Shops: Mon–Sat 9–7 or 10–8. Some close Mon and an hour at lunch.

● Museums: National museums close on Tue, municipal museums on Mon. Individual opening hours vary.

● Main dailies are *Le Monde* (serious, centrist), *Libération* (left-wing) and *Le Figaro* (right-wing).

● For weekly listings of cultural events, buy a copy of *Pariscope* (pariscope.fr; the most popular listings magazine) or *L'Officiel des Spectacles* (offi.fr).

● Central newspaper kiosks and newsagents stock European dailies (widely available on the day of issue) and *USA Today*.

● Visit trouverlapresse.com to find out exactly where you can buy your favorite publication.

SENSIBLE PRECAUTIONS

● Pickpockets are active, particularly in busy bars, flea markets, cinemas, the Métro, railroad stations and the airport.

● Ticket touts operate at train and Métro stations. Buy from machines or ticket kiosks.

● Keep the numbers of your traveler's checks separate from the checks.

● It is important to make a declaration at a local *commissariat* (police station) to claim losses on your insurance.

● Women are generally safe traveling alone or together, although the same risks apply as in any city in western Europe. Deal with any unwanted attention firmly and politely. Avoid the Métro late at night.

TELEPHONES

● Public phone booths are not numerous. Most phone booths use Orange cards (*télécarte* for 50 or 120 units), sold at post offices, *tabacs* or main Métro stations.

● To call France from the US, dial 011 33, then leave out the first zero. To call the US from France dial 00 1, followed by the number.

● To call France from the UK, dial 00 33—omit the first zero from the number. To call the UK from France, dial 00 44—omit the first zero.

● All numbers in the Île-de-France, including Paris, start with 01 unless they are premium rate, when they start with 08; some are toll-free.

● Numbers in the French provinces begin with: 02 Northwest, 03 Northeast, 04 Southeast, 05 Southwest.

TICKETS

● The Paris Museum Pass (parismuseum pass.com) gives access to 59 museums and monuments. It is valid for two, four or six consecutive days. You can buy it online or at tourist offices, museums and Fnac stores.

● Paris Passlib' is available from tourist offices across Paris. It offers entry to over 50 museums and monuments plus reductions at other attractions, a river cruise, Big Bus tour and all public transportation costs for a period of two, three or five consecutive days.

Words and Phrases

BASIC VOCABULARY

oui/non	*yes/no*
s'il vous plaît	*please*
merci	*thank you*
excusez-moi	*excuse me*
pardon	*I'm sorry*
bonjour	*hello, good morning*
bonsoir	*good evening*
au revoir	*goodbye*
de rien/avec plaisir	*you're welcome*
parlez-vous anglais?	*do you speak English?*
je ne comprends pas	*I don't understand*
combien?	*how much?*
trop cher	*too expensive*
je voudrais…	*I'd like…*
où est/sont…?	*where is/are…?*
ici/là	*here/there*
tournez à gauche/droite	*turn left/right*
tout droit	*straight on*
quand?	*when?*
aujourd'hui	*today*
hier	*yesterday*
demain	*tomorrow*
combien de temps?	*how long?*
à quelle heure?	*at what time?*
à quelle heure ouvrez-vous/fermez-vous?	*what time do you open/close?*
avez-vous…?	*do you have…?*
une chambre simple	*a single room*
une chambre double	*a double room*
avec/sans salle de bains	*with/without bathroom*
le petit déjeuner	*breakfast*
le déjeuner	*lunch*
le dîner	*dinner*
c'est combien?	*how much is this?*
puis-je réserver une table	*I'd like to book a table*
une bouteille/un verre de…	*a bottle/glass of…*
acceptez-vous des cartes de crédit?	*do you take credit cards?*
j'ai besoin d'un médecin/dentiste	*I need a doctor/dentist*
pouvez-vous m'aider?	*can you help me?*
où est l'hôpital?	*where is the hospital?*
où est le commissariat?	*where is the police station?*

NUMBERS

un	1
deux	2
trois	3
quatre	4
cinq	5
six	6
sept	7
huit	8
neuf	9
dix	10
onze	11
douze	12
treize	13
quatorze	14
quinze	15
seize	16
dix-sept	17
dix-huit	18
dix-neuf	19
vingt	20
vingt-et-un	21
trente	30
quarante	40
cinquante	50
soixante	60
soixante-dix	70
quatre-vingts	80
quatre-vingt-dix	90
cent	100
mille	1,000

MONTHS

janvier	*January*
février	*February*
mars	*March*
avril	*April*
mai	*May*
juin	*June*
juillet	*July*
août	*August*
septembre	*September*
octobre	*October*
novembre	*November*
décembre	*December*

Index

We would like to thank the following photographers, companies and picture libraries for their assistance in the preparation of this book:

2i Paris Tourist Office/Marc Bertrand; 2ii, 2iii AA/K Blackwell; 2iv Hemis/Alamy; 2v © Paris Tourist Office – Photographer Sarah Sergent; 3i, 3ii, 3iii, 3iv, 4 AA/K Blackwell; 5 © Paris Tourist Office/Sarah Sergent; 6/7t AA/K Blackwell; 6/7ct PARAMOUNT/THE KOBAL COLLECTION; 6/7cb THE KOBAL COLLECTION; 6/7b Kristjan Porm/Alamy; 7ct AA/K Blackwell; 7cb MGM/THE KOBAL COLLECTION; 8/9t, 8c AA/K Blackwell; 8/9b AA/K Paterson; 9cl AA/K Blackwell; 9cb © Paris Tourist Office – Photographer Amélie Dupont; 10l AA/K Blackwell; 10r The Bridgeman Art Library; 11 Keystone/Getty Images; 12, 14, 15tl, 15cl, 15tr, 15cr AA/K Blackwell; 16l Centre Pompidou; 16tr AA/T Souter; 16/17 Susana Vázquez; 17l AA/C Sawyer; 17tr Susana Vázquez; 17cr Centre Pompidou; 18t, 18b, 19tl, 19cl, 19r, 20l, 20/21t, 20c, 21c AA/K Blackwell; 21r AA/M Jourdan; 22t, 22cl, 22cr, 23t, 23c AA/K Blackwell; 24l AA/M Jourdan; 24tr AA; 24cr, 25tl, 25cl, 25r AA/K Blackwell; 26/27 age fotostock/Alamy; 27tr AA/C Sawyer; 27cr, 28l AA/K Blackwell; 28/29t GAUTIER Stephane/SAGAPHOTO.COM/Alamy Stock Photo; 28/29tc, 29t, 29c AA/K Blackwell; 30 AA/C Sawyer; 30/31t AA/K Paterson; 30/31c, 31t AA/M Jourdan; 31c AA/K Paterson; 32l, 32/33t AA/M Jourdan; 32/33c AA/J Tims; 33t The Bridgeman Art Library; 33c Susana Vázquez; 34 AA/J Tims; 35tl AA/K Blackwell; 35c Hemis/Alamy Stock Photo; 36l AA/M Jourdan; 36/7t Chloé Vollmer–Lo/Musée Picasso; 36/7b Chloé Vollmer–Lo/Musée Picasso; 37r AA/P Kenward; 38, 38/39 AA/K Blackwell; 39t imageBROKER/Alamy; 39cr AA/K Blackwell; 40 AA/K Blackwell; 41tl Giraudon/The Bridgeman Art Library; 41cl The Art Archive/Alamy; 41r Hemis/Alamy; 42 AA/K Blackwell; 42/43t AA/M Jourdan; 42/43c AA/K Blackwell; 43t AA/B Rieger; 43cl, 43cr, 44, 45l AA/K Blackwell; 45r, 46/47, 47l AA/K Blackwell; 47r AA/M Jourdan; 48 AA/T Souter 48/49t AA/K Blackwell; 48/49c AA/M Jourdan; 49, 50l, 50r, 50/51, 51l AA/K Blackwell; 51t AA/M Jourdan; 51c AA/K Blackwell; 52 AA/C Sawyer; 53l AA/P Kenward; 53t Paris Tourist Office/Marc Bertrand; 53c Andrew Duke/Alamy; 54l AA/K Blackwell; 54r Glenn Harper/Alamy; 54/55 Jon Arnold Images Ltd/Alamy; 55 JOHN KELLERMAN/Alamy; 56, 56/57t, 56c, 57l AA/K Blackwell; 57tr, 57cr AA/J Tims; 58–59 RossHelen editorial/Alamy; 60, 60/61t, 60/61c, 61t, 61c, 62, 63tl AA/K Blackwell; 63c AA/M Jourdan; 63tc AA/K Blackwell; 63tr Hemis/Alamy; 64, 66l, 66r, 67l, 67r, 68 AA/K Blackwell; 69l AA/C Sawyer; 69r © Paris Tourist Office – Photographer Amélie Dupont; 70l, 70r AA/K Blackwell; 71l JOHN KELLERMAN/Alamy; 71r, 72 AA/K Blackwell; 73l AA/C Sawyer; 73r © Paris Tourist Office/Nicky Bouwmeester; 74 Alexander Krassel/Alamy Stock Photo; 75l claude thibault/Alamy Stock Photo; 75r, 76 AA/K Blackwell; 77l, 77r AA/D Noble; 78l Disney Enterprises, Inc; 78r Disney Enterprises, Inc; 79 AA/D Noble; 80 Hemis/Alamy; 82t AA/K Blackwell; 82b AA/J Tims; 83t, 83b, 86i AA/K Blackwell; 86ii imageBROKER/Alamy; 86iii AA/K Blackwell; 86iv AA/M Jourdan; 86v, 87 © Paris Tourist Office – Photographer Amélie Dupont; 88t Christophe Testi/Alamy; 88b, 89t AA/K Blackwell; 89b AA/C Sawyer; 92i, 92ii AA/K Blackwell; 92iii AA/K Paterson; 92iv, 92v, 92vi AA/K Blackwell; 94t AA/M Jourdan; 95 AA/K Blackwell; 98i Centre Pompidou; 98ii Musée Picasso/Chloé Vollmer–Lo; 98iii © Paris Tourist Office – Photographer– Agnès Moreau; 100, 101t, 101b, 104i, 104ii, 104iii AA/K Blackwell; 104iv AA/J Tims; 104v AA/K Blackwell; 104vi AA/M Jourdan 106t © Paris Tourist Office – Photographer Daniel Thierry; 106b AA/M Jourdan; 107t AA/J Tims; 107b AA/P Enticknap; 110t AA/T Souter; 110b AA/J Tims; 11l AA/K Blackwell; 111r, 112t AA/M Jourdan; 112c AA/K Blackwell; 112b AA/M Jourdan; 113t AA/K Blackwell; 113c © Paris Tourist Office – Photographer Marc Bertrand; 116i, 116ii, 116iii, 116iv, 117 AA/K Blackwell; 118 © Paris Tourist Office – Photographer Sarah Sergent; 120/121t Paris Tourist Office/Marc Bertrand; 120/121ct Paris Tourist Office/David Lefranc; 120cb, 120/121cb, 120/121b, 125 AA/C Sawyer; 127, 128, 130 AA/K Blackwell; 132/133t, 132ct Paris Tourist Office/David Lefranc; 132/133ct AA/K Blackwell; 132/133cb Paris Tourist Office/Amélie Dupont; 133cb AA/P Enticknap; 132b AA/K Paterson; 133b, 140 AA/K Blackwell; 142i AA/C Sawyer; 142ii, 142iii, 142iv, 144, 147, 148 AA/K Blackwell; 150 AA/C Sawyer; 152 AA/K Blackwell; 154i Hemis/Alamy Stock Photo; 154ii Courtesy of Dorchester Collection; 154iii AA/C Sawyer; 154iv Courtesy of Dorchester Collection; 160 AA/K Blackwell.

Every effort has been made to trace the copyright holders, and we apologize in advance for any unintentional omissions or errors. We would be pleased to apply any corrections in a following edition of this publication.

Paris 25 Best

WRITTEN BY Fiona Dunlop and Neville Walker
UPDATED BY Lindsay Bennett
SERIES EDITOR Clare Ashton
COVER DESIGN Jessica Gonzalez
DESIGN WORK Tom Whitlock and Liz Baldin
IMAGE RETOUCHING AND REPRO Ian Little

ISBN 978-1-64097-330-5

SIXTEENTH EDITION

Printed and bound in China by 1010 Printing Group Limited.

10 9 8 7 6 5 4 3 2 1

A05743
Maps in this title produced from mapping data supplied by Global Mapping, Brackley, UK © Global Mapping and data available from openstreetmap.org © under the Open Database License found at opendatacommons.org
Transport map © Communicarta Ltd, UK

Titles in the Series